Three
Dimensional
Type

Three Dimensional Type

Three-dimensional typography has always held a special allure in the world of design. It has the power to captivate and engage viewers in a way that traditional two-dimensional type cannot. With the advent of 3D design and the growing popularity of this creative technique, the realm of typography has been transformed into a playground of imagination and innovation. This showcase, 'Three Dimensional Type', provides an entirely new compilation that celebrates the endlessly-creative world of three-dimensional typography.

Jon Dowling
Counter-Print

This book showcases the unlimited possibilities that emerge when letterforms transcend their conventional boundaries and become objects of digital art or crafted models that can be touched and experienced in real life. The transformation of a simple letter into something unexpected and fantastical is, in the right hands, truly surprising. Each project featured in the book invites you to explore the fusion of the familiar and the extraordinary, providing a vast array of inspiration for graphic designers.

One of the most remarkable aspects of the three-dimensional type trend is its freedom from rules and guidelines. Some projects are more obviously typographic and some move towards the realm of illustration. With basic design software, any existing font can be infused with the captivating allure of three dimensions and can take on an illustrative form. The work we are mainly concerned with showcasing here are the designs that transcend mere legibility and delve into the realm of pure imagination.

While three-dimensional typography has a history dating back to the 1960s, we owe its recent resurgence to advances in design software. These technological advancements have breathed new life into the craft, allowing designers to push the boundaries of perception and what can be achieved with typography. It's a really exciting time for typography in design and the next few years will no doubt see this artform's popularity continue to rise.

Incorporating three-dimensional typography into design projects can help inject either a palpable sense of realism, or even playfulness and humour, that can elevate the work. As AI and realistic effects continue to gain momentum, it is no surprise that 3D typography has become an integral part of this transformative design movement. Although not primarily intended for legibility, the playful nature of the three-dimensional type on show within this book makes it an irresistible design trend worth exploring and documenting.

When we look at the three-dimensional typography collated here, we discover that texture is often the key to unlocking its full potential. UK-based animator, creative director, and 3D artist Thomas Burden master-fully captures the essence of tactile experiences through his typographic works. His creations of words and letters contain textures that are so exquisitely rendered that they encourage us to reach out and touch them.

The future of 3D typography in graphic design seems to hold limit-less possibilities. The integration of AI and advanced software tools like Cinema 4D is revolutionising our industry, propelling it toward uncharted territory. In this ever-evolving landscape, it is challenging to predict precisely how AI will shape the realm of three-dimensional typography. Yet, one thing is for certain: the impact will be significant and long lasting.

In 'Three Dimensional Type', we have curated a collection of our favourite works by talented designers such as Snask, João Varela, Studio-Spass and Zuzanna Rogatty. Their contributions showcase a diverse range of techniques and approaches, from drop shadows and typographic signage to AI-generated typography and hand lettering. Each featured work is accompanied by insightful project descriptions, offering a glimpse into the creative thinking behind the designs.

This book also provides captioning containing the fonts and software utilised in each project, which will hopefully equip readers with the necessary tools to embark on their own three-dimensional typography explorations. It serves as a wellspring of inspiration, a guide through uncharted territories and a celebration of the extraordinary possibilities that await those who embrace the mind-bending world of three-dimensional typography.

We hope this book provides inspiration and helps you transform your design work into something out of the ordinary. The future is calling and, seemingly, it is a realm where letters come alive, words transcend their confines and typography will evolve into an extraordinary, unexpected, surprising art form, full of intelligence and wit.

The future of 3D typography in graphic design seems to hold limitless possibilities. The integration of AI and advanced software tools like Cinema 4D is revolutionising our industry, propelling it toward uncharted territory. In this ever-evolving landscape, it is challenging to predict precisely how AI will shape the realm of 3D type.

4

João Varela
DutchScot
PAZ MIAMOR
A Practice for Everyday Life
DixonBaxi

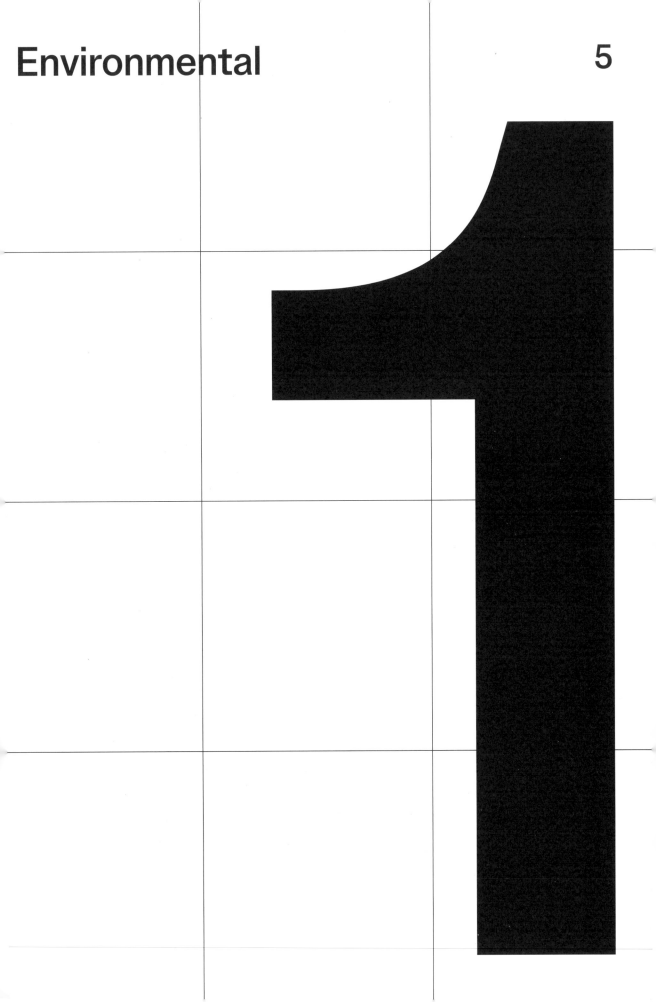

6

COMPANY
João Varela
URL
joaoistyping.com
FONTS
Custom
SOFTWARE
Adobe Illustrator
and hand-painted

2 de Maio

This football court is in Lisbon, Portugal, in the '2 de Maio' neighbourhood. The neighbourhood got its name because on May 2nd 1974, right after the revolution that overthrew the authoritarian Portuguese regime, hundreds of people took over the then-unfinished buildings and occupied them for years to come. The important date and name were celebrated with a big and impactful orthogonal typographical composition in shades of blue, inspired by the local architecture, the Tagus River and the open blue skies of Lisbon.

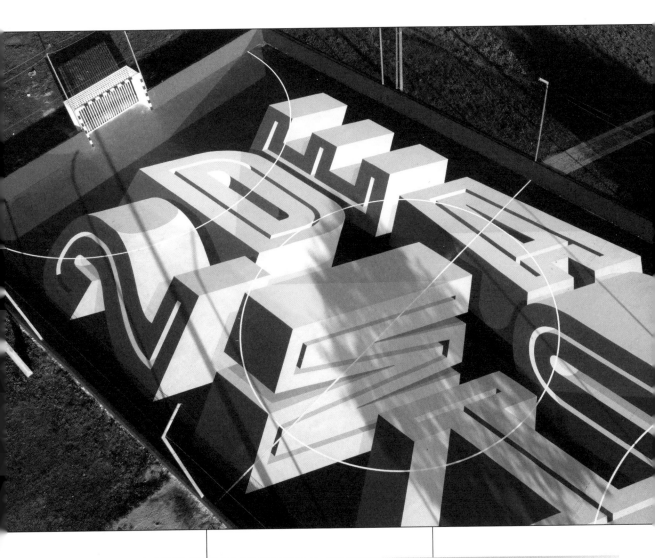

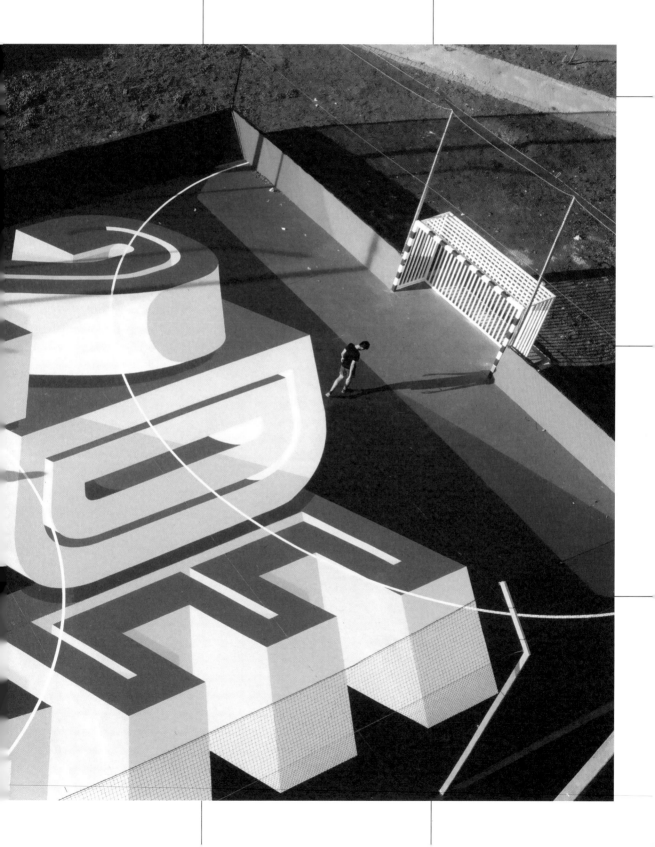

Design District

Located in North Greenwich, London, 'Design District' is a new home for the creative industries, defined by its striking and varied architecture.

A wayfinding and signage system was needed that felt befitting of this creative community. The solution celebrates the eclectic nature of the District, using the distinctive form and material of each building as a starting point and key wayfinding component. The playful use of 'pinning' and layering of materials, as well as colour and typography, are used throughout as a nod towards the creative nature of the District's residents and their processes.

COMPANY
DutchScot
URL
dutch.scot
FONTS
Mabry
SOFTWARE
Adobe InDesign
Adobe Illustrator
Adobe Photoshop

Monocle Type

Monocle Type is an experimental typographic project inspired by old monocles and their refractive lenses. By passing a magnifying glass over any object, what happens inside changes and gives rise to something new and unpredictable.

The digital objects and environments were recreated, mixing the 3D language with animation. The integration of the real world with the digital was developed by working with light, texture and shadow. The final compositions, where digital meets real world, were recreated in Barcelona. The result is a mix of graphic design, 3D and photography, which creates a feeling of something new and old simultaneously.

COMPANY
PAZ MIAMOR
URL
pazmiamor.com
FONTS
Monocle Type
SOFTWARE
Adobe Illustrator
Adobe Photoshop
Cinema 4D

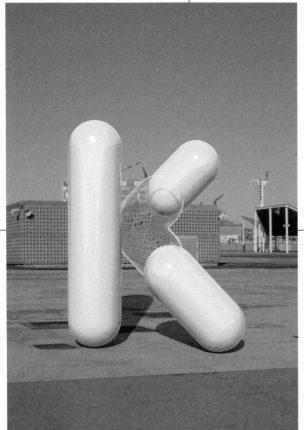

nature
and the synthesis
of the arts

'Léger, Pierre Jeanneret and I used to go to the Mediterranean beaches... We would fill our backpacks with treasure: pebbles, bits of stones, lumps of wood riddled with holes, but above all wood all smoothed and washed by the sea... We called it our Art Brut.'

In the mid-1930s, Perriand turned away from the machine aesthetic she had previously embraced. Her work began to take on the organic forms she found in nature. She photographed trees and stones, and collected rocks from beaches. Drawn to the sensual qualities of wood, she began designing free-form tables.

During the Second World War, Perriand spent two formative years in Japan, where she'd been invited by the government to advise on how the country's traditional craft products could be modernised. She immersed herself in the local way of life. This exposure to the types, flexible spaces of Japanese houses – in particular, the sense of ordered emptiness – would influence the rest of her career.

When she returned to Tokyo years later, Perriand staged an exhibition called Proposal for a Synthesis of the Arts in 1955. It was a manifesto of sorts, demonstrating her belief that architecture, design and art should work together to create a harmonious interior. Here, industrial metal shelving slung with crafted wooden tables and chairs were shown surrounded by modernist paintings and tapestries by her friends Fernand Léger and Le Corbusier.

Charlotte Perriand

'Charlotte Perriand: The Modern Life' was a major retrospective of the pioneering designer's work, held at the Design Museum in 2021. It presented the breadth of Perriand's influential practice – spanning the modernist machine aesthetic, her exploration of natural forms, modular furniture designs and major architectural projects.

Custom modular lettering was created for the exhibition titles, produced in bent tubular steel – a material and process that Perriand often worked with in her furniture design. Section texts are screen-printed directly onto the gallery walls, while bespoke folded metal captions are integrated into surfaces and structures built up of large, concrete blocks.

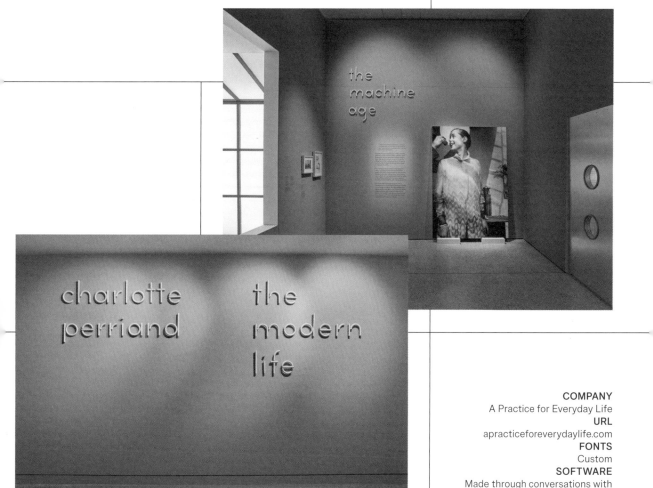

COMPANY
A Practice for Everyday Life
URL
apracticeforeverydaylife.com
FONTS
Custom
SOFTWARE
Made through conversations with
the fabricator, Chop Chop
PHOTOGRAPHY
Thomas Adank
© A Practice for Everyday Life

Regent's Place

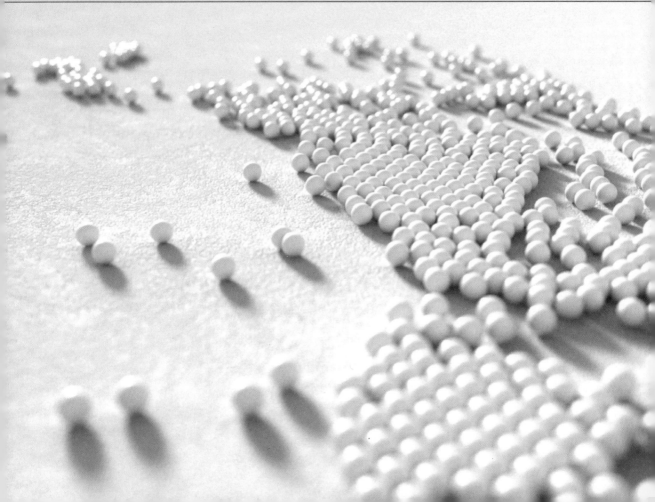

Regent's Place

This brand identity by DixonBaxi is for Regent's Place, a dynamic destination in the centre of London.

The identity reflects the unique advantages of Regent's Place by highlighting its location at the crossroads of three iconic districts: the Knowledge Quarter, Camden, and Fitzrovia. A compelling mix that brings together arts and science, research and creativity. The three districts intersect to form the 'R' symbol.

Designed to be transparent and almost disappear, the symbol frames different perspectives and provides a space for the community, local stories, and an ever-changing neighbourhood.

COMPANY
DixonBaxi
URL
dixonbaxi.com
FONTS
Gradual
Gotham
SOFTWARE
Adobe InDesign
Adobe After Effects
Adobe Illustrator
Adobe Photoshop
Procreate

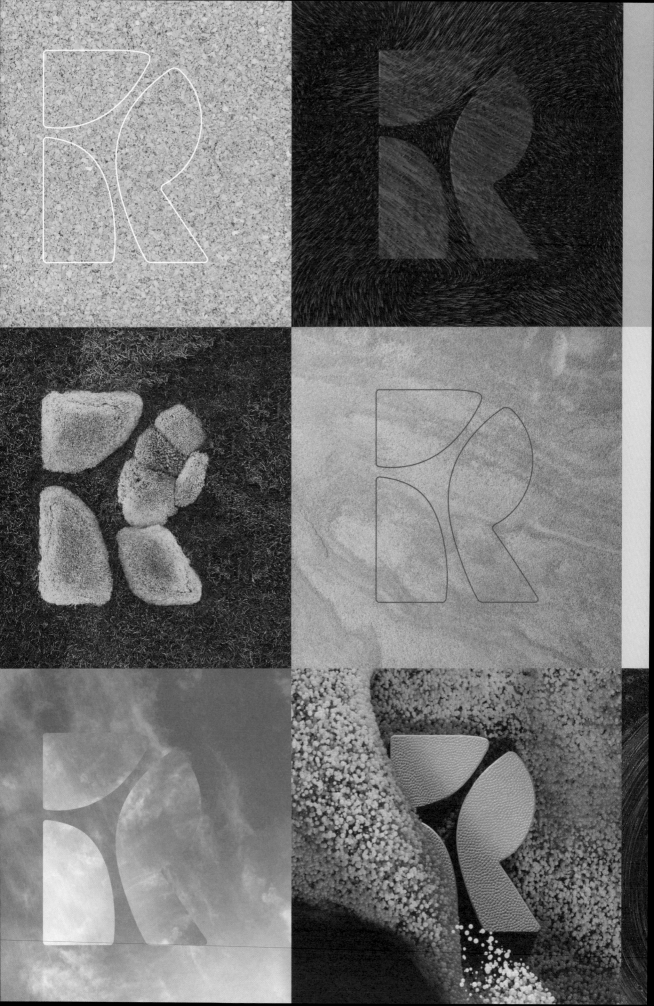

DixonBaxi
HDU²³ Lab
Snask
StudioSpass
Everyday Practice
Pupila
Erich Brechbühl [Mixer]
Jo Cutri Studio
ITAL/C
Basora
HelloMe
Ariane Spanier

Paddington Central

In a move that showcases the constant innovation and transformation of Paddington Central, DixonBaxi partnered with British Land to create a placemaking brand that celebrates the vibrant canalside community in Central London.

The ethos of the brand is rooted in the idea of 'launching into a different every day' reflecting the dynamic and ever-evolving nature of Paddington Central.

DixonBaxi crafted a new symbol that reacts and adapts to the day-to-night energy paired with the fluidity of the water. With its curved flourish, the 'P' acts as a 'living sundial', the form only revealed by its elongated illumination. As the extended form of the 'P' rotates around, it graphically illuminates different facets of Paddington Central through a changing day-to-night palette, bespoke photography and live action of the water. In motion, the form comes alive as a reflection, with its edges rippling as if seen on the water.

The 'P' symbol is used flexibly across the brand, while the logo lock-up provides a sophisticated signature in its vibrant red.

COMPANY
DixonBaxi
URL
dixonbaxi.com
FONTS
Maax Micro
Atlas Typewriter
SOFTWARE
Adobe InDesign
Adobe After Effects
Adobe Illustrator
Adobe Photoshop
Procreate

The ethos of the brand is rooted in the idea of 'launching into a different every day,' reflecting the dynamic and ever-evolving nature of Paddington Central.

Dappled sunlight

Whispering reeds

Jewel-like water

That soothes the mind.

Explore
Question
Unwind
Taste
Converse
Delight
Rest
Invite
Wander
Reunite
Learn
Savour

Paddington
Central

SYMBIOSIS
OF LIGHT
一次与光的共生

2023.9.27-3.2

深圳会展中心
SHENZHEN
CONVENTION AND
EXHIBITION CENTER

Eugenio
WallpaperSTORE

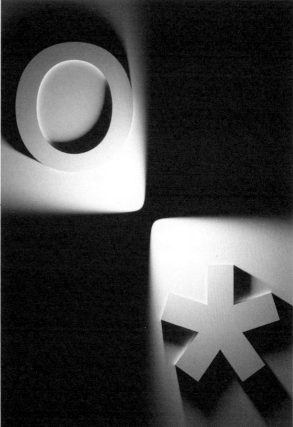

Symbiosis of Light

These posters were designed with the theme of 'Symbiosis of Light' for the joint fair by German luxury lighting brand Occhio and WallpaperSTORE*.

Teaser and official versions were designed, combining the brand elements and exhibition information of both parties with the product features. The elements are expressed in the form of light and shadow to reflect the style of the exhibition's content and the theme of symbiosis.

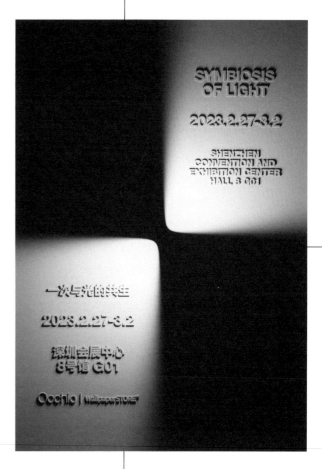

COMPANY
HDU²³ Lab
URL
hdu23.design
FONTS
Helvetica
Alibaba-PuHuiTi
SOFTWARE
Cinema 4D
Houdini

Wallbaby

This branding was created by Snask in a personal and flirtatious manner for a curated online poster store.

COMPANY
Snask
URL
snask.com
FONTS
Grauna
SOFTWARE
Adobe Creative Suite

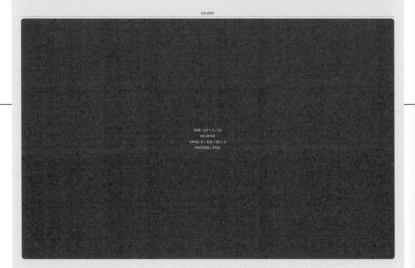

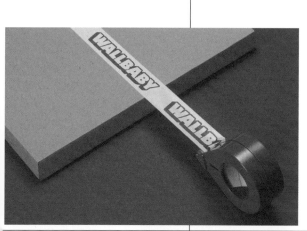

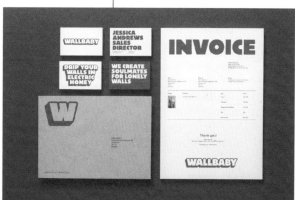

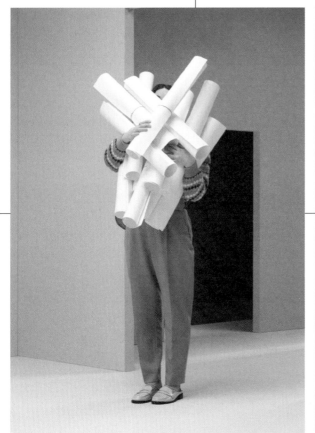

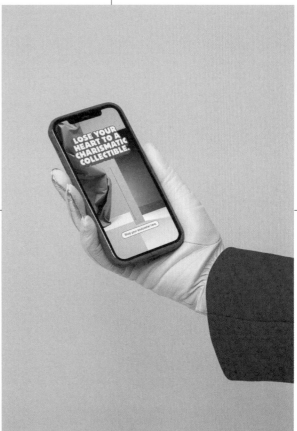

West Side Stories

COMPANY
StudioSpass
URL
studiospass.com
FONTS
Favorit
SOFTWARE
Adobe InDesign

West Side Stories is an architecture festival in the form of an exhibition, several lectures and a publication. The project's aim is to illuminate the celebrated urban renewal of the Oude Westen district in Rotterdam.

Inspired by the postmodern aesthetics of Rotterdam's urban renewal period (1970–1990) StudioSpass designed this colourful and dynamic identity, as well as the book and an exhibition.

The clean typographic grid served as a basis for the playful design approach. StudioSpass decided to cover the base grid with a graphic language inspired by Trespa plating aesthetics, one of the most iconic materials from this time period. Low in maintenance it was often a cheap solution used to give older building a new look.

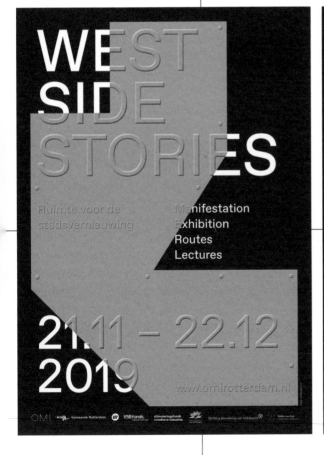

Aqua Paradiso Catalogue

Aqua Paradiso is an exhibition that imagines a positive future through life, birth, healing, regeneration and recovery under the theme of ocean and ecology. Everyday Practice tried to visualise the concept of 'healing and recovery of water in a mythical/religious sense'. They designed the key visual by borrowing the phenomenon of Anthropocene and the landscape of climate crisis that it causes as a graphic motif.

The cover of the exhibition catalogue symbolises the life, healing and recovery potential of water. The inside of the book is designed in a similar way to how the works are displayed in the exhibition.

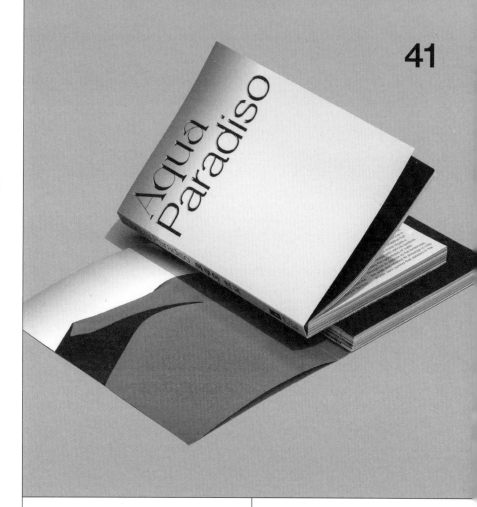

COMPANY
Everyday Practice
URL
everyday-practice.com
FONTS
Neue Haas Grotesk
Sandoll Gothic Neo
Voyage
Suisse
SOFTWARE
Adobe Illustrator
Adobe Photoshop
Adobe InDesign

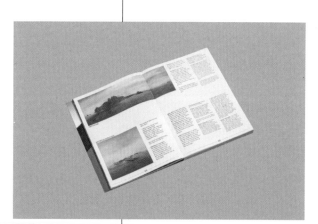

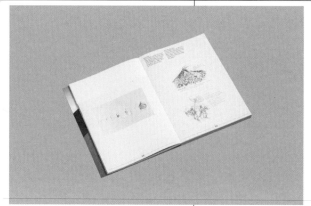

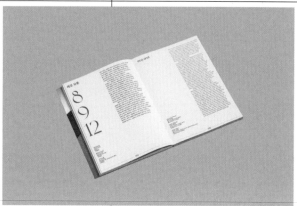

2022 ACC FOCUS

아쿠아 천국

Aqua Paradiso

2022.
6. 9.—9. 12.

ACC Creation Space 3 & 4, Asia Culture Center
국립아시아문화전당 문화창조원 복합3·4관

권혜원
김태은
닥드정
리경
리우 위
마리안토
부지현
빠키
아드리앵 M & 클레어 B
에코·오롯
이 이란

Hyewon Kwon
Tae-Eun Kim
Dakd Jung
Ligyung
Liu Yu
Maryanto
BOO Jihyun
Vakki
Adrien M & Claire B
eco orot
Yee I-Lann

주최·주관   국립아시아문화전당
Hosted & Organized by Asia Culture Center

아쿠아 천국

Aqua Paradiso

2022.
6. 9.—9. 12.

ACC Creation Space 3 & 4, Asia Culture Center
국립아시아문화전당 문화창조원 복합3·4관

권혜원	Hyewon Kwon
김태은	Tae-Eun Kim
닥드정	Dakd Jung
리경	Ligyung
리우 위	Liu Yu
마리안토	Maryanto
부지현	BOO Jihyun
빠키	Vakki
아드리앵 M & 클레어 B	Adrien M & Claire B
에코 오롯	eco orot
이 이란	Yee I-Lann

주최·주관 국립아시아문화전당
Hosted & Organized by Asia Culture Center

OLI!

Convenience stores are a common thing in pretty much all Latin American cities (big or small) and Costa Rica has plenty of them. These 'mini supermarkets' sell all the essential products we need to go with our day-to-day lives.

Oli! was founded to become a fresh alternative for those who enjoy nightlife. The store is in a vibrant neighbourhood, full of bars, restaurants and night clubs. The brand mimics the youthful spirit and attitude of the visitors that pack this area, through solid shapes and catchy colours.

COMPANY
Pupila
URL
pupila.co
Fonts
Futura
SOFTWARE
Adobe Illustrator
PHOTOGRAPHY
Mateos Muñoz

Nine Years Neubad

This poster was created for the nine year anniversary of the cultural interim use of the old municipal indoor swimming pool in Lucerne.

That year, the focus of the anniversary was on families with children. That's why Erich Brechbühl decided to create a numner '9' out of black and white building blocks.

COMPANY
Erich Brechbühl
[Mixer]
URL
erichbrechbuhl.ch
FONTS
Brown
SOFTWARE
Cinema 4D

COMPANY
Erich Brechbühl
[Mixer]
URL
erichbrechbuhl.ch
FONTS
Custom, based
on Compacta
GT Maru
SOFTWARE
Cinema 4D

THEATER AETERNAM SPIELT
TÜR AUF   TÜR ZU
VON   INGRID LAUSUND
25./26. SEPT. 21   20 UHR
THEATERPAVILLON LUZERN

SPIEL FRANZISKA BACHMANN PFISTER
              CHRISTOPH FELLMANN
                   MARCO SIEBER
                  SURAMIRA VOS
REGIE   DAMIÄN DLABOHA
DRAMATURGIE CHRISTOPH FELLMANN
AUSSTATTUNG   ELKE MULDERS
STÜCKRECHTE   SUHRKAMP BERLIN

WWW.   AETERNAM.CH

Door Open Door Closed

Theatre poster designed for a play by Ingrid Lausund in which a door
plays the leading role. Since the designer, Erich Brechbühl, also wanted
to stage this door as the main character on the poster, he tried to show
it both open and closed. This gave him the idea to implement this in four
panels in order to simulate movement. The resulting white space makes

The concept behind the branding and packaging design was influenced by the brand owners of Thanks Darl and their love for 70s music. This theme was adopted throughout the design in the fonts and colour palettes used.

Darl Bar

Darl Bars are a healthy treat, handmade in the Byron Bay region using premium organic ingredients sourced from local farmers. The bars are handmade with activated, slow roasted chickpeas, organic seeds and fragrant spice blends, baked with a touch of organic brown rice syrup and macadamia oil to create a soft, melt in your mouth 'darliciousness'.

The concept behind the branding and packaging design was influenced by the brand owners of Thanks Darl and their love for 70s music. This theme was adopted throughout the design in the fonts and colour palettes used.

Each flavour has its own unique colour palette and flavours include Caramel Pecan, Cinnamon Almond, Dark Chocolate & Hazelnut, Dutch Cocoa & Sourberry and Turmeric.

COMPANY
Jo Cutri Studio
URL
jocutristudio.com
FONTS
PAG Trust
Recoleta
Arial Rounded
SOFTWARE
Adobe Creative Suite

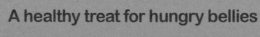

A healthy treat for hungry bellies

DARL BAR

Cinnamon Almond

Plant Based
Organic Seeds
Source of Protein

THANKS DARK

DARK

Dark Chocolate & Hazelnut

Pla
Organic
Source of F

Sou

THS

A healthy treat for hungry bellies

DARL BAR

Turmeric

Plant Based
Organic Seeds
Source of Protein

40g

S DARK

THANKS DARK

DAR

Cinnamon Almond

A hea

reat for hungry bellies

BAR

Plant Based
Organic Seeds
Source of Protein

40g

ate

A healthy treat for hungry bellies

DARL BAR

Dutch Cocoa Sour Berry

THANKS DARK

Plant Based
Organic Seeds
Source of Protein

Caramel Pecan
THANKS DARL
Dutch Cocoa
& Sour Berry
hungry bellies
Organic Seeds
Source of Protein
40g
A healthy treat for hungry bellies
THANKS DARL
DARL BAR
Dark Chocolate
& Hazelnut
Plant Based
Organic Seeds
Source of Protein
40g
A healthy treat for hungry bellies
DARL BAR
Plant Based
Organic Seeds
Source of Protein
40g
Pecan
THANKS DARL

JB SKRUB

When it comes to body care for tween boys there's not a whole lot of options out there that speak to them. That's where JB SKRUB comes in.

ITAL/C were tasked with everything from naming to brand identity to packaging. Their task was to create a brand that is, 'vibrant, fun, has no ego, and also would stand out amongst all the brooding and way too serious competitors that crowd the shelves of many a store'.

COMPANY
ITAL/C
URL
italic-studio.com
FONTS
Custom
SOFTWARE
Adobe Illustrator
Glyphs

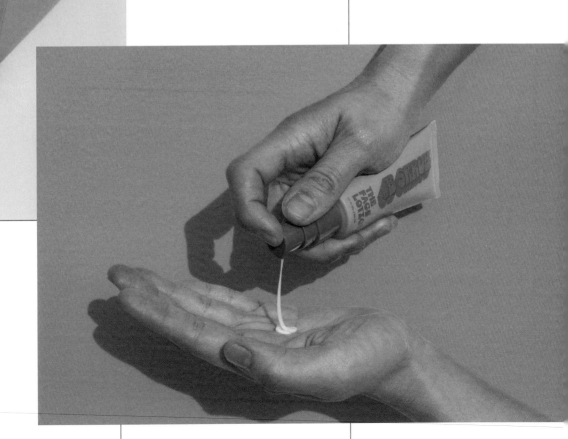

Their task was to create a brand that's vibrant, fun, has no ego, and also would stand out amongst all the brooding and way too serious competitors that crowd the shelves of many a store.

Since it's a super-refreshing beverage, Basora wanted to create a logo that feels fresh, lively and with a cool, retro touch.

Splash

Basora had a fun time designing the logo for Nomad Coffee's cold coffee drink. Since it's a super-refreshing beverage, they wanted to create a logo that feels fresh, lively and with a cool, retro touch. Taking inspiration from the movie 'Splash', starring Tom Hanks and Daryl Hannah, they developed a lettering style reminiscent of those 80s logos. The result is a logo that brings together a sense of freshness, energy and retro vibes.

COMPANY
Basora
URL
basora.info
FONTS
Sneaker Script
SOFTWARE
Adobe Illustrator
PHOTOGRAPHY
Enric Badrinas

COMPANY
HelloMe
URL
hellome.studio
FONTS
HM Artus
SOFTWARE
Adobe InDesign
Glyphs 2

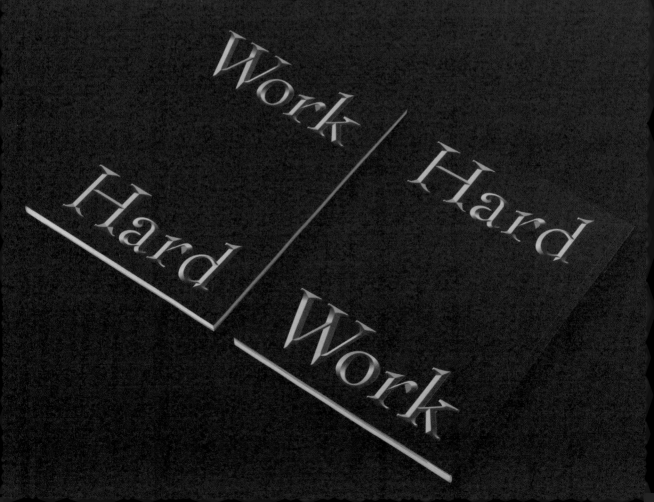

Berlin Art Prize Catalogue

In addition to working on the visual identity of the Berlin Art Prize 2016, themed 'Hard Work, Work Hard', HelloMe designed a publication accompanying the exhibition.

    The 88 page publication is conceptualised around the theme of labour and showcases artworks by the nominees, shot in the studios where they were created. The book features contributions by writers including Rainald Goetz, Dr. Helen Hester, Lorena Juan and Chloe Stead, amongst others.

    The thread-stitched publication is printed on two contrasting paper stocks and features a high-gloss cover with large, embossed typography on the front and back.

The 88 page publication is conceptualised around the theme of labour and showcases artworks by the nominees, shot in the studios where they were created.

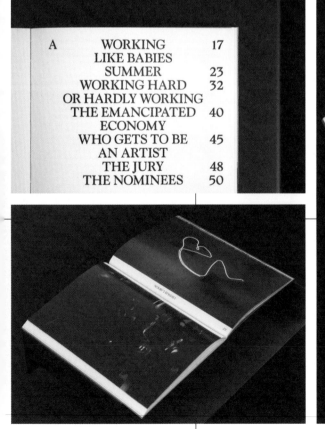

The Lives of Things

Poster for an art exhibition by Swedish artists Björn Hegardt and Theo Ågren at Kunsthall Ålesund. The art installation showed objects mixing three-dimensional black holes and blobs, overgrowing pedestals, tables and everyday objects. The custom typography referenced the behaviour and shapes of the objects.

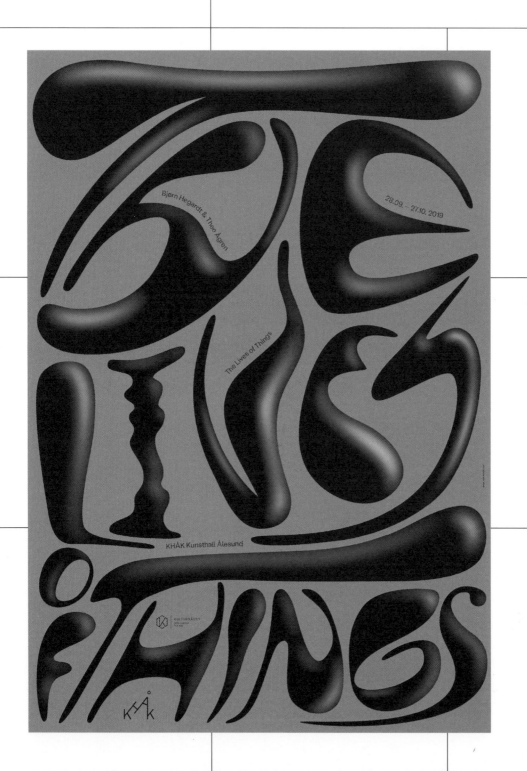

COMPANY
Ariane Spanier
URL
arianespanier.com
FONTS
Custom
SOFTWARE
Adobe Illustrator

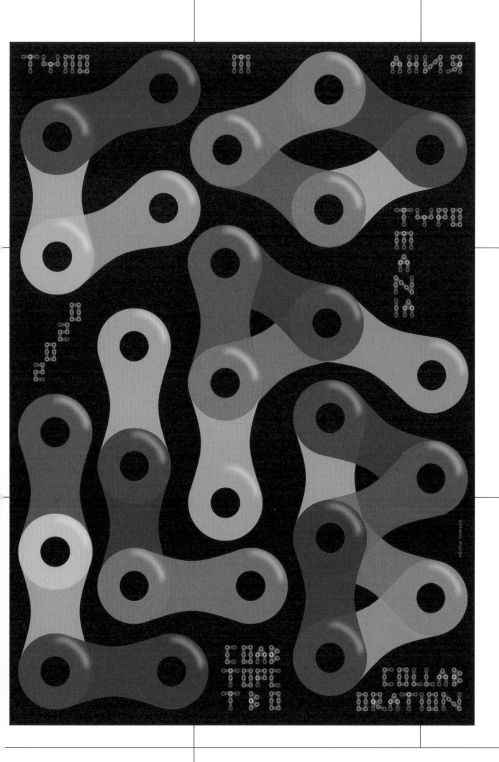

Typomania 'Collaboration'

COMPANY
Ariane Spanier
URL
arianespanier.com
FONTS
Custom
SOFTWARE
Adobe Illustrator

Contribution to a project on collaboration for the typography festival Typomania, taking place in Moscow in 2020. The poster design was later animated by a young designer from Moscow, both poster and animation were exhibited at the festival.

gggrafik design
Everyday Practice
AKU
THINGS I DID
Erich Brechbühl [Mixer]
Matúš Hnát
Ward Heirwegh
SPGD
HDU^{23} Lab
Surfaces
OMSE

The Cyberpunk Experience

This visual concept/poster by gggrafik design for 'Cyberpunk Symposium' at ZKM Karlsruhe was inspired by Rutger Hauer's 'Tears in Rain' monologue in 'Bladerunner'.

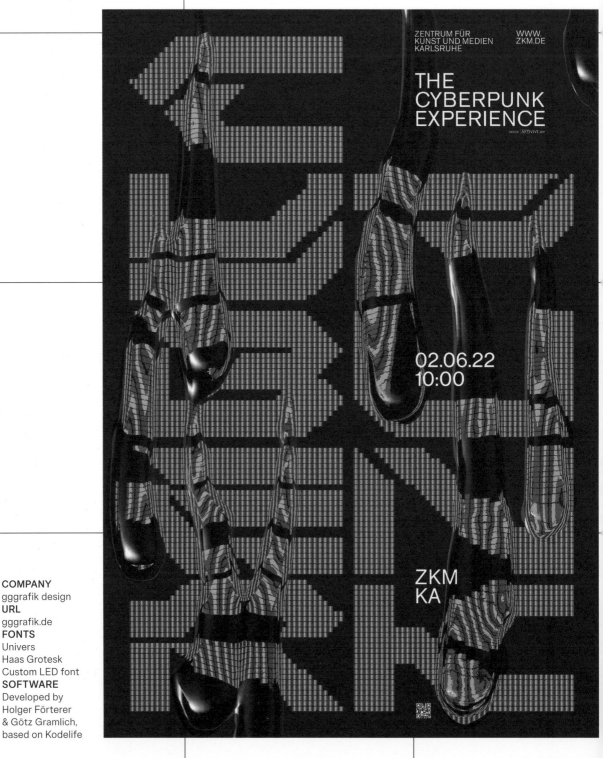

COMPANY
gggrafik design
URL
gggrafik.de
FONTS
Univers
Haas Grotesk
Custom LED font
SOFTWARE
Developed by
Holger Förterer
& Götz Gramlich,
based on Kodelife

Open Up!

'Open Up!' was planned as an online exhibition of 30 contemporary artists, representing Korea and China, to commemorate 2021–2022, the year of cultural exchange between the two countries and the 30th anniversary of their diplomatic relations.

COMPANY
Everyday Practice
URL
everyday-practice.com
FONTS
Cinderblock
Sandoll Gothic Neo
SOFTWARE
Adobe Illustrator
Adobe Photoshop
Adobe InDesign
Cinema 4D

TMW 2018

The visual identity of the TMW festival's jubilee edition is based on the concept of change, a shift to a new era. This is expressed through a custom typeface (created by Aimur Takk) and the optical distortions generated with the help of glass tubes. Together with a strong colour scheme (red, blue, gold) this created a dynamic and easily usable system that helped the festival's communication stand out.

COMPANY
AKU
URL
aku.co
FONTS
Custom
SOFTWARE
Adobe Creative Suite

The visual identity of the TMW festival's jubilee edition is based on the concept of change, a shift to a new era. This is expressed through a custom typeface (created by Aimur Takk) and the optical distortions generated with the help of glass tubes.

TMW10!
2–8 April
2018

Kadri Kont-Kontson,
Operations Manager
TMW 2018

NAVER VIBE

COMPANY
Everyday Practice
URL
everyday-practice.com
FONTS
Suisse Int'l
SOFTWARE
Adobe Illustrator
Adobe Photoshop
Cinema 4D

Everyday Practice designed a series of playlist cover images for NAVER music streaming platform 'VIBE'. Based on the concept and the mood of the selected songs, they freely composed graphic elements in a square canvas.

'Hidden Masterpiece' is a playlist containing hidden masterpieces of various genres. The combination of a blurred layer and illustrations that reinterpret the characteristics of the genre, metaphorically express that the masterpieces are hidden. The geometrically processed alphabet was glass-textured to create a blurred layer and the genre's name was enlarged to create a consistent layout system.

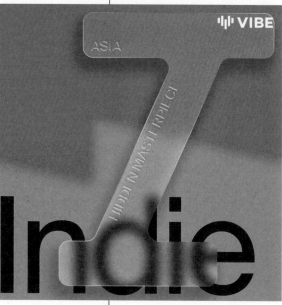

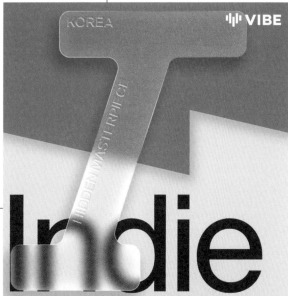
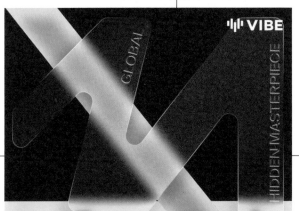
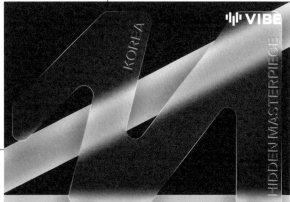

ON AIR

We breathe in and out for over 20,000 times a day. Do we know what we are breathing? 'ON AIR' is a public project to re-orient public consciousness to the air we breathe, and also a part of an ongoing journey to explore how creativity and collaboration can bring new perspectives to environmental, urban and well-being issues. The public could learn about air quality, air pollution and ways to improve air quality through participatory exhibitions and educational activities.

COMPANY
THINGS I DID
URL
thingsidid.org
FONTS
GT Maru
Neue Montreal
SOFTWARE
Adobe Illustrator
Adobe Photoshop
Adobe Dimension

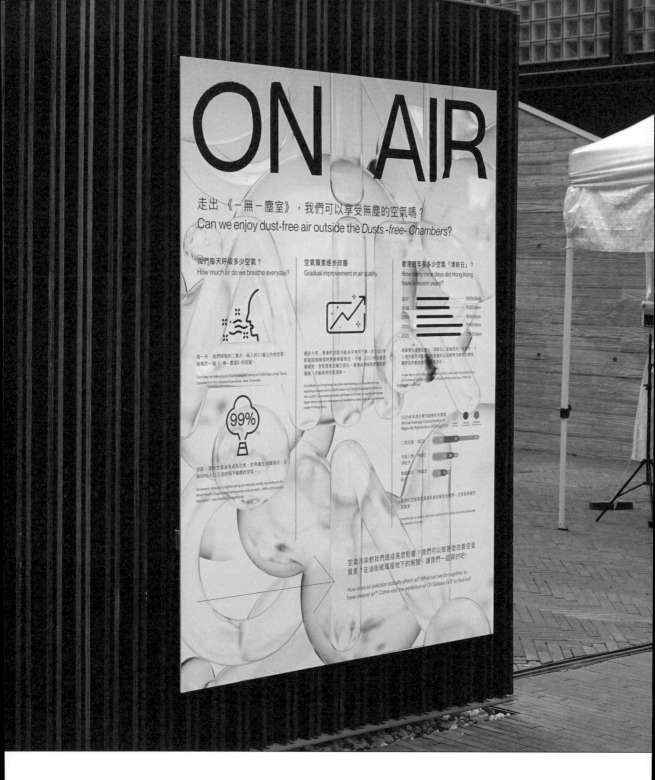

ON AIR is a public project to re-orient public consciousness to the air we breathe, and also a part of an ongoing journey to explore how creativity and collaboration can bring new perspectives to environmental, urban and well-being issues.

2022 VIDEO BITES

'VIDEO BITES' is an exhibition on video art. It's aim was to boost the consumption of video and media works by considering ways where individuals can own the works through collecting and by the lowering of the purchase threshold of content to increase the self-sustainability of artists.

Everyday Practice intuitively conveys the meaning of the title by visualising 'bytes', the basic unit of data, as a 3D object. They gathered objects to represent the initials 'V' and 'B' and tried to symbolically express the flexibility and scalability of video and media works.

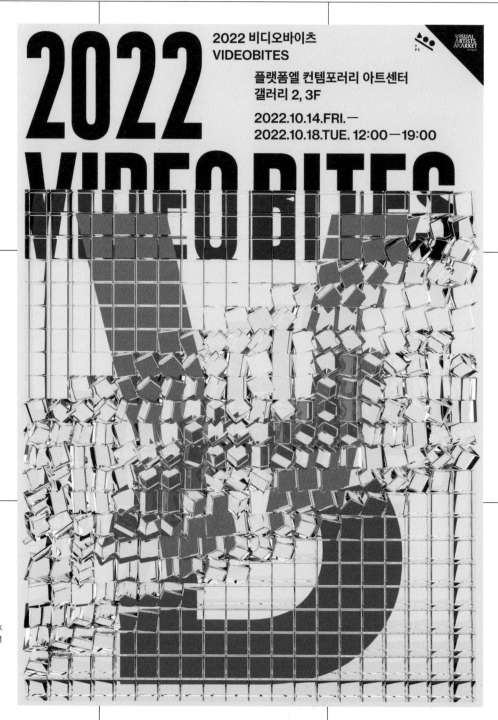

COMPANY
Everyday Practice
URL
everyday-practice.com
FONTS
Plak LT
Neue Haas Grotesk
Sandoll Gothic Neo1
SOFTWARE
Adobe Illustrator
Adobe Photoshop
Adobe InDesign
Cinema 4D

COMPANY
Erich Brechbühl
[Mixer]
URL
erichbrechbuhl.ch
FONTS
FS Elliot Pro
SOFTWARE
Cinema 4D

Kieler Woche 2023

This poster is Erich Brechbühl's proposal for the 2023 edition of 'Kieler Woche' in Kiel/Germany, the biggest sailing event in Europe. The history of the Kieler Woche posters is full of great solutions. Many are based on the abstraction of a sail onto a triangle. But Kieler Woche seemed much wilder when Erich Brechbühl researched it. That's why the designer decided to focus on the movement of the water and the lights of the festival reflecting on it.

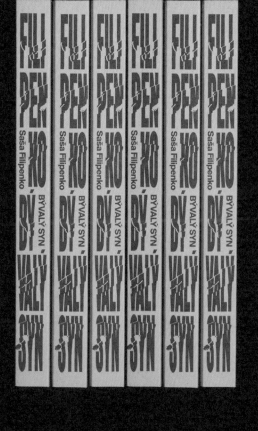

Sasha Filipenko:
The Ex-Son (Bývalý syn)

The typographic solution on this book cover is connected with the embossed silhouette of the reclining figure – the main character of this satire about a Belarusian plunged into a coma by Alexander Lukashenko's pro-Russian regime. A huge tragedy occurs, in which sixteen-year-old Francisk is accidentally injured. He falls into a coma and doesn't come out of it for years. After ten years, Francisk wakes up. However, he finds himself in a country where absolutely nothing has changed in ten years. It is ruled by the same man, young people are leaving, every protest is suppressed. Will Francisk find his place in this country?

COMPANY
Matúš Hnát
URL
behance.net/matushnat
Fonts
Monopol
Suisse Int'l
Arnhem
SOFTWARE
Adobe InDesign
Adobe Illustrator

Bâtard is a yearly festival for emerging performance and theatre artists that takes place at Beursschouwburg in Brussels. Each edition features a different constellation of curators that decide the theme of the festival together. For the 2017 edition 'Into the pores of the brain' was chosen as the tagline. The slogan gave birth to two design elements that were used in most of the festival's applications: seeing through things (visual or literal) and the vague idea of brainwaves. Holes were punched in booklets, brainwaves were used to separate elements and even brain fog was suggested: the slogan started to deform as the festival neared its end.

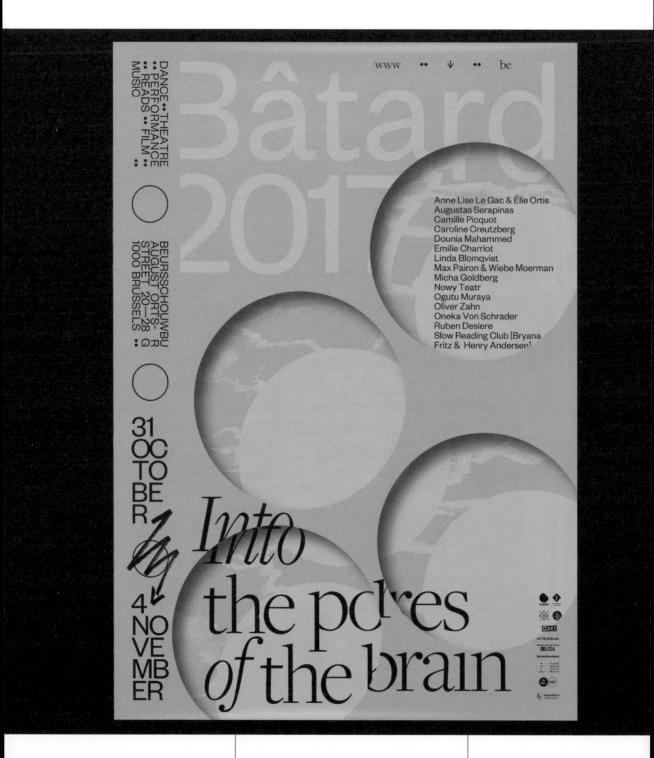

COMPANY
Ward Heirwegh
URL
wardheirwegh.com
FONTS
Founders Grotesk
Freight Display
SOFTWARE
Adobe InDesign

Bâtard 2017

www •• ↓ •• be

DANCE •• THEATRE
:: PERFORMANCE
:: READS :: FILM ::
MUSIC ::

BEURSSCHOUWBU
AUGUST ORTS-
STREET 20—28 G
1000 BRUSSELS ::

31 OCTOBER — 4 NOVEMBER

Anne Lise Le Gac & Élie Ortis
Augustas Serapinas
Camille Picquot
Caroline Creutzberg
Dounia Mahammed
Emilie Charriot
Linda Blomqvist
Max Pairon & Wiebe Moerman
Micha Goldberg
Nowy Teatr
Ogutu Muraya
Oliver Zahn
Oneka Von Schrader
Ruben Desiere
Slow Reading Club [Bryana
Fritz & Henry Andersen]

Into
the pores
of the brain

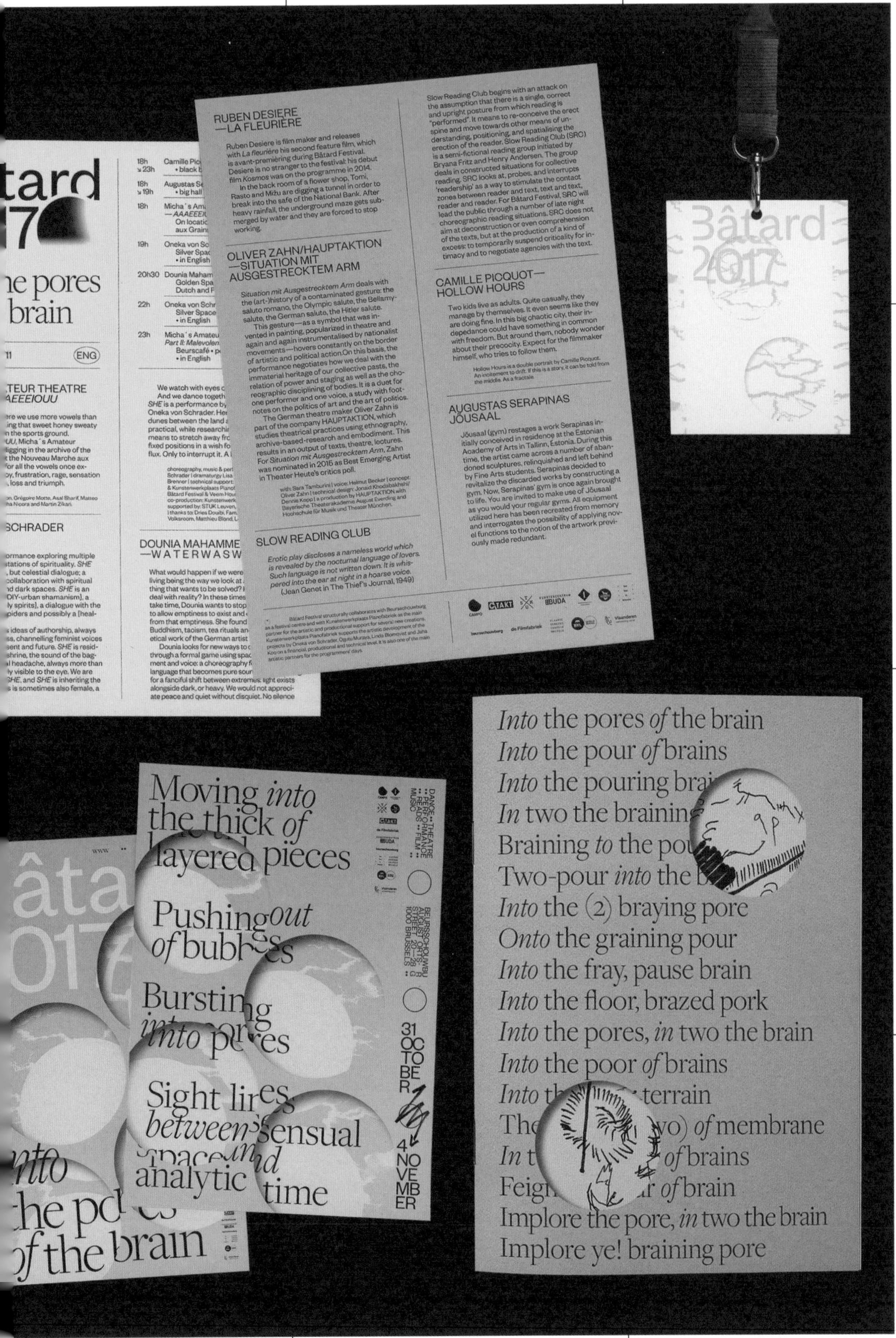

RUBEN DESIERE — LA FLEURIÈRE

Ruben Desiere is film maker and releases with *La fleurière* his second feature film, which is avant-premièring during Bâtard Festival. Desiere is no stranger to the festival: his debut film Kosmos was on the programme in 2014.

In the back room of a flower shop, Tomi, Rasto and Micha are digging a tunnel in order to break into the safe of the National Bank. After heavy rainfall, the underground maze gets submerged by water and they are forced to stop working.

OLIVER ZAHN/HAUPTAKTION — SITUATION MIT AUSGESTRECKTEM ARM

Situation mit Ausgestrecktem Arm deals with the (art-)history of a contaminated gesture: the Olympic salute, the Bellamy-saluto romano, the German salute, the Hitler salute.

This gesture—as a symbol that was invented in painting, popularized in theatre and again and again instrumentalised by nationalist movements—hovers constantly on the border of artistic and political action. On this basis, the performance negotiates how we deal with the immaterial heritage of our collective pasts, the relation of power and staging as well as the choreographic disciplining of bodies. It is a duet for one performer and one voice, a study with footnotes on the politics of art and the art of politics.

The German theatre maker Oliver Zahn is part of the company HAUPTAKTION, which studies theatrical practices using ethnography, archive-based-research and embodiment. This results in an output of texts, theatre, lectures. For *Situation mit Ausgestrecktem Arm*, Zahn was nominated in 2015 as Best Emerging Artist in Theater Heute's critics poll.

with: Sara Tamburini | voice: Helmut Becker | concept: Oliver Zahn | technical design: Jonald Khodabakhshi/Dennis Kopp | a production by HAUPTAKTION with Bayerische Theaterakademie August Everding and Hochschule für Musik und Theater München.

SLOW READING CLUB

Erotic play discloses a nameless world which is revealed by the nocturnal language of lovers. Such language is not written down. It is whispered into the ear at night in a hoarse voice
(Jean Genet in The Thief's Journal, 1949)

Slow Reading Club begins with an attack on the assumption that there is a single, correct and upright posture from which reading is "performed." It means to re-conceive the erect spine and move towards other means of understanding, positioning, and spatialising the erection of the reader. Slow Reading Club (SRC) is a semi-fictional reading group initiated by Bryana Fritz and Henry Andersen. The group deals in constructed situations for collective reading. SRC looks at, probes, and interrupts 'readership' as a way to stimulate the contact zones between reader and text, text and text, reader and reader. For Bâtard Festival, SRC will lead the public through a number of late night choreographic reading situations. SRC does not aim at deconstruction or even comprehension of the texts, but at the production of a kind of excess: to temporarily suspend criticality for intimacy and to negotiate agencies with the text.

CAMILLE PICQUOT— HOLLOW HOURS

Two kids live as adults. Quite casually, they manage by themselves. It even seems like they are doing fine. In this big chaotic city, their independance could have something in common with freedom. But around them, nobody wonder about their precocity. Expect for the filmmaker himself, who tries to follow them.

Hollow Hours is a double portrait by Camille Picquot. An incitement to drift. If this is a story, it can be told from the middle. As a fractale.

AUGUSTAS SERAPINAS JOUSAAL

Jousaal (gym) restages a work Serapinas intitialy conceived in residence at the Estonian Academy of Arts in Tallinn, Estonia. During this time, the artist came across a number of abandoned sculptures, relinquished and left behind by Fine Arts students. Serapinas decided to revitalize the discarded works by constructing a gym. Now, Serapinas' gym is once again brought to life. You are invited to make use of Jousaal as you would your regular gyms. All equipment utilized here has been recreated from memory and interrogates the possibility of applying novel functions to the notion of the artwork previously made redundant.

Bâtard Festival structurally collaborates with Beursschouwburg as a festival centre and with Kunstenwerkplaats Pianofabriek as the main partner for the artistic and production support for several new creations. Kunstenwerkplaats Pianofabriek supports the artistic development of the projects by Oneka von Schrader, Ogutu Muraya, Linda Blomqvist and Juha Kuja as a financial, productional and technical level. It is also one of the main artistic partners for the programme's days.

(left column, partial)

18h — Camille Pic[...] 23h • black b[...]

18h — Augustas Se[...] 19h • big hall

18h — Micha´s Amateur[...] —AAAEEE[...] On location, aux Grain[...]

19h — Oneka von Sc[...] Silver Spac[...] • in English

20h30 — Dounia Maham[...] Golden Spa[...] Dutch and F[...]

22h — Oneka von Schr[...] Silver Space[...] • in English

23h — Micha´s Amateur[...] Part II: Malevolen[...] Beurscafé • p[...] • in English

Bâtard 2017

the pores of the brain

11 (ENG)

[AMA]TEUR THEATRE —AAEEEIOUU

[...]ere we use more vowels than [...]ing that sweet honey sweaty [...]n the sports ground. [...]UU, Micha´s Amateur [...]gging in the archive of the [...]the Nouveau Marche aux [...]or all the vowels once ex[...]oy, frustration, rage, sensation [...], loss and triumph.

[...]on, Grégoire Motte, Axel Sharif, Mateo [...]ha Nicora and Martin Zikari.

[VON] SCHRADER

[...]ormance exploring multiple [...]stations of spirituality. *SHE* [...], but celestial dialogue; a [...]collaboration with spiritual [...]nd dark spaces. *SHE* is an [...]DIY-urban shamanism), a [...]ly spirits), a dialogue with the [...]piders and possibly a [heal-

[...]s ideas of authorship, always [...]s, channelling feminist voices [...]sent and future. *SHE* is resid[...]shrine, the sound of the bag[...]al headache, always more than [...]y visible to the eye. We are [...]GHE, and *SHE* is inheriting the [...]s is sometimes also female, a

DOUNIA MAHAMME[...] —WATERWASW[...]

What would happen if we were [...] living being the way we look at [...] thing that wants to be solved? [...] deal with reality? In these times [...] take time, Dounia wants to stop[...] to allow emptiness to exist and [...] from that emptiness. She found [...] Buddhism, tacism, tea rituals an[...] etical work of the German artist[...]

Dounia looks for new ways to c[...] through a formal language using spac[...] ment and voice a choreography f[...] language that becomes pure soun[...] for a fanciful shift between extremism[...] alongside dark, or heavy. We would not appreci[...] ate peace and quiet without disquiet. No silence

We watch with eyes [...] And we dance togeth[...] *SHE* is a performance by [...] Oneka von Schrader. Her[...] dunes between the land a[...] practical, while research[...] means to stretch away fr[...] fixed positions in a wish fo[...] flux. Only to interrupt it. A I[...]

choreography, music & per[...] Schrader | dramaturgy Lisa [...] Brenner | technical support: [...] & Kunstenwerkplaats Pianof[...] Bâtard Festival & Veem Hou[...] co-production: Kunstenwerk[...] supported by: STUK Leuven, [...] | thanks to: Dries Douibi, Fam[...] Volksroom, Matthieu Blond, L[...]

Bâtard 2017

www [...]

Moving *into* the thick of layered pieces

DANCE THEATRE PERFORMANCE FILM MUSIC

Pushing *out of* bubbles

Bursting *into* pores

Sight lines *between* sensual space *and* analytic time

BEURSSCHOUWBURG STREET 20 1 26 G 1000 BRUSSELS

31 OCTOBER — 4 NOVEMBER

[...]nto [...]he p[...] of the brain

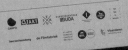

Into the pores *of* the brain
Into the pour *of* brains
Into the pouring brai[...]
In two the braining
Braining *to* the pou[...]
Two-pour *into* the b[...]
Into the (2) braying pore
Onto the graining pour
Into the fray, pause brain
Into the floor, brazed pork
Into the pores, *in* two the brain
Into the poor *of* brains
Into th[...] terrain
The[...] wo) *of* membrane
In t[...] *of* brains
Feign[...]r *of* brain
Implore the pore, *in* two the brain
Implore ye! braining pore

Segma

SPGD were asked to create a type specimen for TDF. The concept was based around celebration and the opening of presents. This was conveyed through the use of various effects. The cover represents lava balloons, whilst the inside plays with a sand-like effect that was blown away revealing what was underneath. This contrast, between the typeface and effects, was used to show the typeface's flexibility and ability to appeal to a broader market.

COMPANY
SPGD
URL
sp-gd.com
FONTS
Sigma
SOFTWARE
Adobe Photoshop
Adobe InDesign

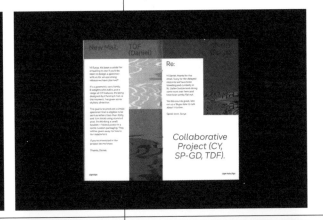

Segma

Segma Typeface by Christoph York (U.K)
for The Designers Foundry™ (NZ).
Specimen designed by SP-GD (AU).
Dimensions: 95x165mm. © 2018.

TheDesignersFoundry.com

'DMZ Art Project' is a project that asks what DMZ means to us living in the present and introduces the answers through the works of artists. The artists who participated in the exhibition captured the traces of confrontation between South and North Korea in the DMZ, the nature of the DMZ without human hands, and the people living in recognition of the confrontation between South and North Korea. Everyday Practice has designed title lettering using barbed wire across South and North Korea as a graphic motif for more than 70 years, and tried to implicitly express the project's theme through a key visual that harmonises the complementary colours.

COMPANY
Everyday Practice
URL
everyday-
practice.com
FONTS
Halver Stencil
Sandoll Gothic
NeoCond
SOFTWARE
Adobe Creative Suite

Bravo Design

'Bravo Design' is a pop-up shop by WallpaperSTORE* hoping to help independent designers promote their design products through Wallpaper's influence in the design community and fans. This poster is designed for Bravo Design's pop-up at JC Plaza, a luxury mall in Shanghai.

HDU[23] Lab express the brand elements of the partners in the form of gold bullion and use the concept of vending machines to convey the original intention of this event – paying for good design. The poster is presented in motion and static forms.

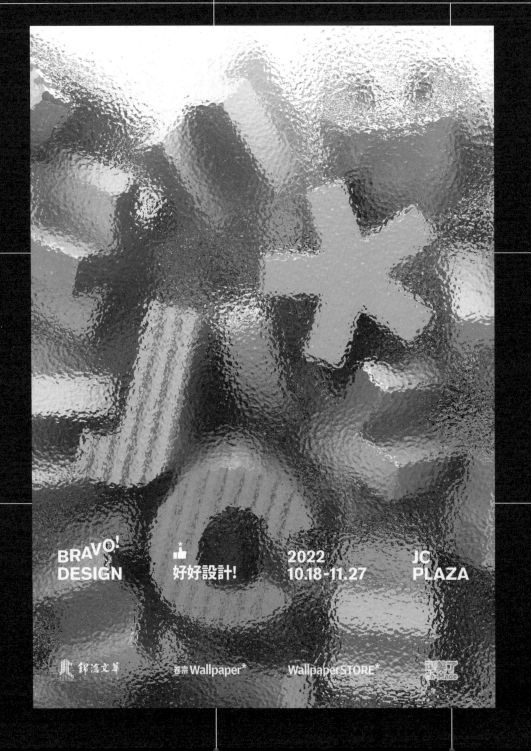

COMPANY
HDU[23] Lab
URL
hdu23.design
FONTS
Akzidenz Grotesk
SOFTWARE
Blender

Audace(s)

Poster for the first 'Audace(s)' festival, dedicated to performing arts through the prism of emerging and student scenes, in Arras (France). The poster's visual draws a parallel between the fragility of the bubble and experimental scenic artistic practices, between the beauty of emergence and the risk of everything bursting at any moment. Silkcreen-printed in three colours by Lézard Graphique.

COMPANY
Surfaces
URL
surfaces-studio.com
FONTS
Untitled Sans
SOFTWARE
Adobe Illustrator
Adobe Photoshop
Adobe InDesign

COMPANY
OMSE
URL
omse.co
FONTS
GT Flexa X Compressed
Apoc
Togalite
Pancho
SOFTWARE
Adobe Illustrator
Adobe Photoshop
Adobe InDesign
Blender

DOJA

Milkman is an international music and events brand based in India. They were launching a gin, which was to be an unexpected fusion of botanicals from India and Japan – a taste of two cultures in one sip. In creating the brand, the idea of mixing became OMSE's inspiration. The name – DOJA – borrowed elements of 'In(do-ja)panese', and felt like it could be native to either country. The logo mixes Japanese, English and Devanagari and the design system mixes up the 'ingredients' – type, illustration and photography – in different ways to create a variety of striking layouts.

Thomas Burden
Marta Cerdà Alimbau
FOREAL
Timea Balo
Daniel Escudeiro

COMPANY
Thomas Burden
URL
wearegrownup.com
FONTS
Custom
SOFTWARE
Adobe Illustrator
Adobe Photoshop
Maxon C4D

Random House NY

Random House in NYC commissioned Thomas Burden to design the cover of Jason Ross' middle grade novel, 'The Amazing Beef Squad: Never Say Die!'.

The book detailed the exploits of a group of middle school friends and the publishers wanted the cover to convey the same feeling of youthful hi-jinx along with notable elements from the plot, in an engaging and contemporary fashion.

Thomas Burden developed a design rooted in playful, bold typography that could have been laid out by the protagonists themselves in a middle school classroom or den. Something he felt that the strong characters in the book would have definitely wanted to have done themselves.

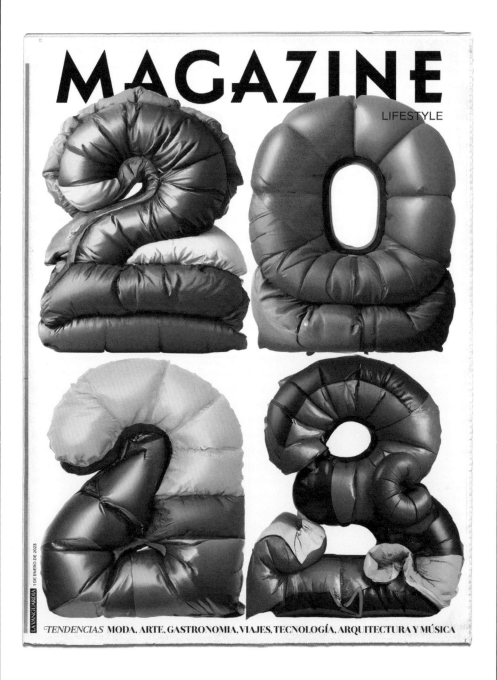

COMPANY
Marta Cerdà
Alimbau
URL
martacerda.com
FONTS
Custom
SOFTWARE
Dall-e2
Let's Enhance
Adobe Photoshop

La Vanguardia

'Magazine' is a weekly paper-magazine supplement to the Sunday edition of 'La Vanguardia'. When Marta Cerdà Alimbau was asked to design the new year's issue cover, dedicated to new trends in 2023, the feared and infamous AI instantly came to mind, as the debate about its place in art and design continues to rage. To answer the ask, she designed the cover and drop cap openers with the assistance of AI. Because, whether we like it or not, Artificial Intelligence is clearly one of the trends for this coming year(s) in every creative field, including typography.

Interview
Thomas Burden

I studied graphic design at Camberwell College of Arts. Although it was a very conceptual course and I left without any tangible design skills of any kind, other than a solid understanding of what makes a good concept. I interned at a couple of ad agencies and then worked for a few design and illustration studios before going freelance as a 3D illustrator in 2014. So for a long while now I've been a graphic designer/art director stuck in the body of an illustrator.

wearegrownup.com

How would you describe your style and creative process?
→　My style has varied over the years as I have always been led by ideas first and foremost, and adapt my style accordingly, although it has mostly been inspired by recollections of toys, type and design from my childhood. In general, I am drawn to bold, playful, kinetic type with a nostalgic bent.

What first inspired you to incorporate 3D typography in your work?
→　It just seems very natural to me to do more and more type work. I started my career at digital illustration agencies, which massively influenced the initial direction of my work and career. I feel like it's been a slow arc back towards my graphic design and typographic roots, as I've always felt more of an art director than an illustrator. Ultimately, I find typography so interesting as a medium in its ability to visually convey and emphasise the sentiment behind the written word by merging language and image. It's a real belt and braces form of communication; clear and concise, but with the emotional power of imagery.

Can you walk us through your workflow when designing 3D type?
→　It varies slightly from project to project but usually I'll moodboard and write up loose ideas before starting to sketch out layouts in Illustrator (when it's not crashing), then I build and animate everything in Cinema 4D and composite and add final touches in After Effects.

THE TRAINLINE

Working with the inhouse team
at the Trainline.com, Thomas Burden
produced a series of different
large-scale versions of the same
copy line for use across an array
of billboard formats at UK train
stations and beyond.

FONTS
Custom
SOFTWARE
Adobe Illustrator
Adobe Photoshop
Cinema 4D

The main challenges with anything 3D is the technical aspects of realising an idea. That's where having a signature style allows you to limit the technical variables and bend concepts to fit within it.

How do you choose the right 3D software for your type projects?

→ Cinema 4D is just a natural choice for my kind of work as its native MoGraph tools are so good. I am really intrigued to learn Unreal Engine when I get the time to, as well as incorporating more AI into the earlier stages of my process.

What are some of the challenges you face when designing 3D type?

→ The main challenges with anything 3D is the technical aspects of realising an idea. That's where having a signature style allows you to limit the technical variables and bend concepts to fit within it.

What do you see as the future of 3D typography in graphic design?

→ In the short term, I hope it holds out a little longer against the AI revolution than standard images, mainly so I can get ahead of the curve a little. AI is going to change a lot about our industry, so it's hard to predict what will happen. Ultimately, ideas and signature styles will still be the most important. I can see AI making trends even more homogenised and faster than ever though.

How do you stay inspired?

→ I am constantly inspired by so many different things that the problem is not being inspired, but choosing which sources of inspiration to follow and which to discount. I have a hard time not to go off on stylistic tangents. Part of being a working freelance creative is sticking to a niche, and that can be hard to do when your eye is drawn to all kinds of other niches.

What are your goals for the future of your company?

→ My main goal now is to just stick to type and to keep it simple, with an eye to doing more branding projects, and to keep a good balance between my work as an artist and as a designer. In general though, I am looking to pivot away from the illustration world and back to more graphic design and branding, as I probably enjoy the conceptual side of things more than the actual execution. That said, I do see a wider scope for the future of my company, but with me acting as an art director on larger projects rather than producing them solely by myself.

JUNG VON MATT

Thomas Burden was one of a number of artists commissioned by agency JVM to illustrate the company's inclusivity statement. Burden brought their words to life in his signature, bouncy, playful style to emulate the warm and welcoming tone of the words. Each piece was then displayed at large-scale in their entrance lobbies.

FONTS
Pirates Gold
Dolly
Custom
SOFTWARE
Adobe Illustrator
Adobe Photoshop
Cinema 4D

JUNG VON MATT SHOULD BE A SPACE WHERE PEOPLE RESPECT ALL EXPERIENCE NO MATTER WHERE THEY COME FROM WHAT THEY BELIEVE HOW THEY THINK WHICH GENDER THEY BELONG TO AND WHO THEY ARE ATTRACTED TO MORE

Quilts for the Homesick Music Fan

This is a self-initiated personal project by Thomas Burden. The designer, keen to explore the aesthetic of quilted typography, believed the symbolism of quilts to be imbued with a strong sense of home. Music lyrics are a great sense of inspiration to him, as they come with an extra level of meaning and emotion for the viewer. So Burden chose, 'three absolute bangers', about home and made sure to select the slightly less obvious lyrics, that still conveyed, 'a sense of hopeful melancholy', through the medium of brightly coloured quilts.

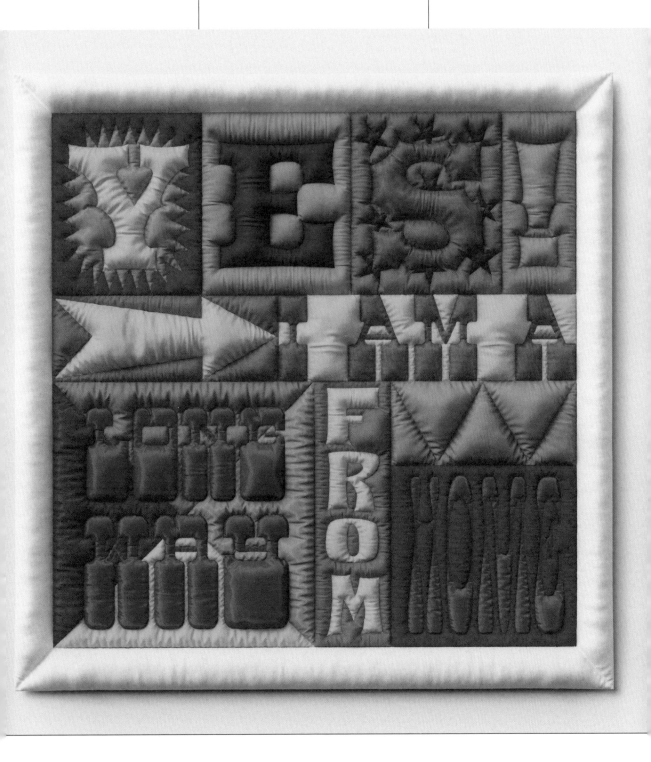

The designer, keen to explore the aesthetic of quilted typography, believed the symbolism of quilts to be imbued with a strong sense of home.

COMPANY
Thomas Burden
URL
wearegrownup.com
SOFTWARE
Adobe Illustrator
Adobe Photoshop
Cinema 4D

FONTS
Bellbottom Laser
Charming Sixties
Discombile
Flowers Kingdom
Gunydrops
Magical Mystery Tour
Superfly
Wonkids

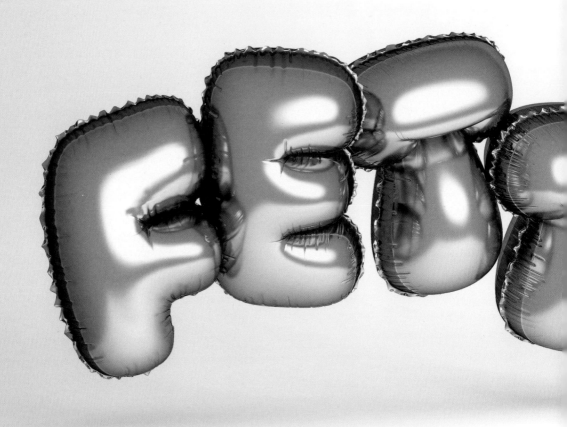

Fettrate

Part of a large set of 3D headlines for an advertising campaign for Base,
a renowned German network provider.

COMPANY
FOREAL
URL
weareforeal.com
FONTS
Custom
SOFTWARE
Cinema 4D
Octane Renderer
Adobe Photoshop

Stylist Magazine

The editors at 'Stylist Magazine' came up with the idea of 'The curse of the office bloat' from conversations in the office about returning to work and starting to move back into our workwear wardrobe and away from leisurewear. This then led to the struggles of dealing with bloat as all women do. What better way to talk about bloat than inflating all the graphics on the cover and making them feel like they're about to pop off the page?

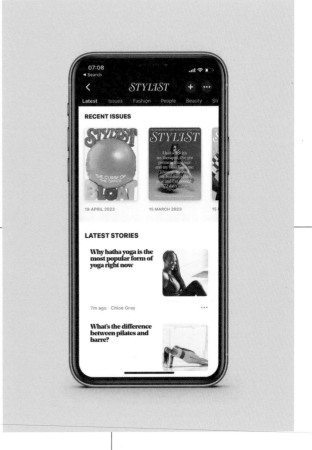

COMPANY
Timea Balo
Follow
madebytimtim.co.uk
FONTS
FuturaFuturis
SOFTWARE
Cinema 4D
Redshift
Adobe Illustrator

Interview
Daniel Escudeiro

I was a classic 'drawing kid' – I drew a lot at home, classmates would ask me for random drawings and I used to draw weird rock band letterings on school tables (much to the disappointment of whoever sat on that table afterwards and had a notebook ruined with graphite). That seems pretty far from whatever I do today with graphic design, but those were the roots. As far as formal education, studying graphic design was always my first and only choice, really.

behance.net/danielescudeiro

How would you describe your style and creative process?

→   I think they are two very different things. My style is, perhaps, a mix of conscious and instinctive balance between contrasts. I often think of (or feel) a design in terms of similarity and difference. Like, which attributes at play are either clearly similar or contrastingly different from each other? To balance opposites and to harmonize similarities. There's no recipe, but I've come to realize this sort of instinct has been present in my work for a while and it is interesting to consciously perceive it. I think that's a line of thought for many things that are visual, from a single glyph to a large visual identity system project, to architecture.

My process, however, is definitely more chaotic, erratic, empirical and malleable. More guts than brains are usually involved (guts are actually kind of second brains, but that's a different topic). As many designers, I truly love the early stages when it's just limitless possibilities and you're creating something out of nothing. I'm a person who's very good with early stages and will easily lose interest for the follow ups and adjustment rounds. That's why personal projects are so fun.

What inspired you to first incorporate 3D typography in your work?

→   I love 3D but I've never been versed in 3D programs – they always seemed too complex and time consuming and I was always involved in other things. Back in early 2022, I saw a reel by Nubia Navarro showing this inflating thing you could suddenly do in Illustrator and that blew my mind. I spent the following weeks deeply experimenting with it, and the result of that was my 2022, 36 Days of Type series.

36 DAYS OF TYPE 2022

This edition of 36 Days of Type marked Daniel Escudeiro's first '3D type' experiments.

ADOBE ILLUSTRATOR SPLASH SCREEN 2023

Adobe approached Daniel Escudeiro to design the custom artwork for the Illustrator splash screen showcasing their new 3D tools. The brief was to create something bold and simple that felt inviting and achievable.

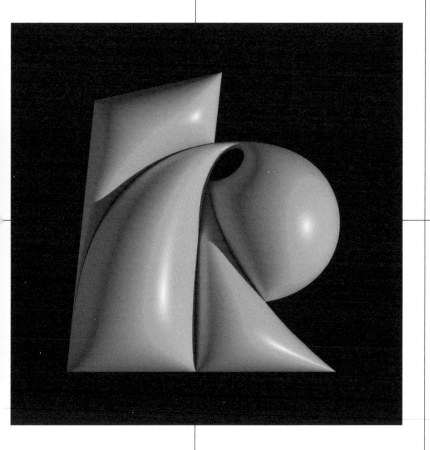

BOTH PROJECTS

FONTS
Custom
SOFTWARE
Adobe Illustrator

LA TIMES

The brief for this 'LA Times' magazine cover lettering project contained the words 'retro futurism', 'early space travel' and an image of the Contemporary Art Museum designed by Brazilian modern architect Oscar Niemeyer, located in Daniel Escudeiro's hometown of Niterói (Brazil). This piece is an amalgamation of Escudeiro's many personal references, such as Brazilian modern architecture, the work of Roberto Burle Marx and Ziraldo, and American 60s/70s display lettering.

BOTH PROJECTS

FONTS
Custom
SOFTWARE
Adobe Illustrator

Can you walk us through your workflow when designing 3D type?

→ As my current 3D skill set is pretty much defined by what I can do in Adobe Illustrator (for now at least), the process often involves just probing though its possibilities and (more interestingly) its limitations. It often leads me to places I would never have thought of through 2D sketches, because once you add that third dimension, crazy new logics come into play. For example, the 'k' in the Adobe Illustrator splash screen could only be designed in that inflated 3D style. Its iteration process of adding/removing weight, refining the curves and overall anatomy only made sense as I took into account the output of the inflated volumes that made up that particular letter design. This may seem obvious to 3D designers, but for me it was interesting to see how some traditional type design rules had to be completely reinterpreted.

What are some of the challenges you face when designing 3D type?

→ It's a game of subverting traditional rules, but at the same time I think it's very important to be aware and conscious of 'classic' type anatomy and construction principles. I think it's interesting when there's a fresh 3D solution built upon all of the centuries-old basis we have for type. If you also consider micro/macro typography, so many of the traditional rules or good practices are based on a flat space, so 3D typography has many ways of exploring its own logic. I really like that. As for constraints, I am still personally bound by the restraints of the 3D I can do right now, which is pretty limited. I'd love to get into actual sculpting and more advanced motion.

What do you see as the future of 3D typography in graphic design?

→ This is a funny question to answer right now, because of artificial intelligence and the big tech gamble on the multiverse. I'm not going to get into it, but AI is obviously disrupting the 'artisanal' way anything visual has been made so far. So there'll be probably more space for 3D in graphic design, made by people who previously wouldn't have the skills to. Things like Illustrator evolving its native 3D also open the door to graphic designers making complex looking 3D they wouldn't know how to do before. The multiverse carries different experiences for type, where one can experience a 3D design in an actual three-dimensional space, rather than a 2D screen (or real life). If enough people will buy expensive, impractical headsets to even experience it, that's the gamble.

How do you stay inspired?

→ I think it's a matter of reaching a place in your mind that is just play. A channel from our messy, complex subconscious to whatever output we're working on. Inspiration runs deep. Everything we experience drains down into a sort of underground river and it is just there somewhere. If you tap into it, that's inspiration.

What are your goals for the future of your company?

→ I'd like to do more personal work and get more into motion and 3D. I'd like to collaborate with awesome people and produce things I couldn't alone. To make physical things and move away from screens more. I don't have hefty, big studio goals. Being able to create cool stuff is what makes me happy.

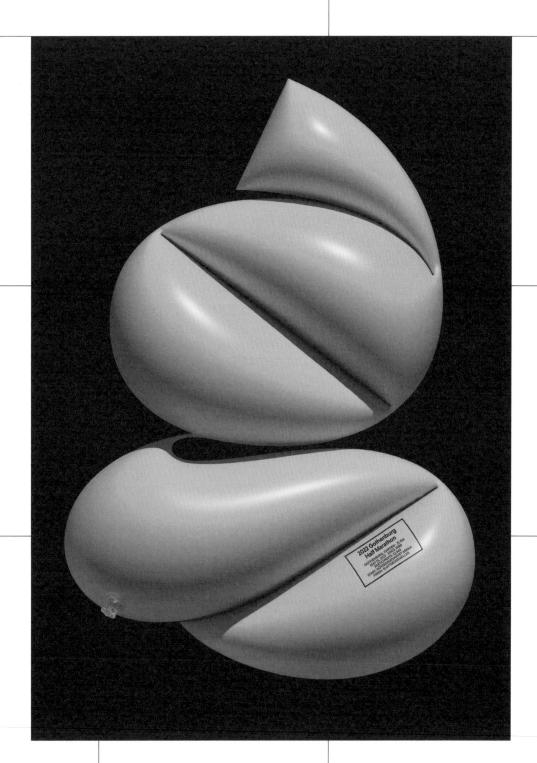

GOTHENBURG MARATHON 2022

Designed after creating the letter 'P' for the 36 DoT project, this was a poster for the summer 2022 Gothenburg half-marathon in Sweden.

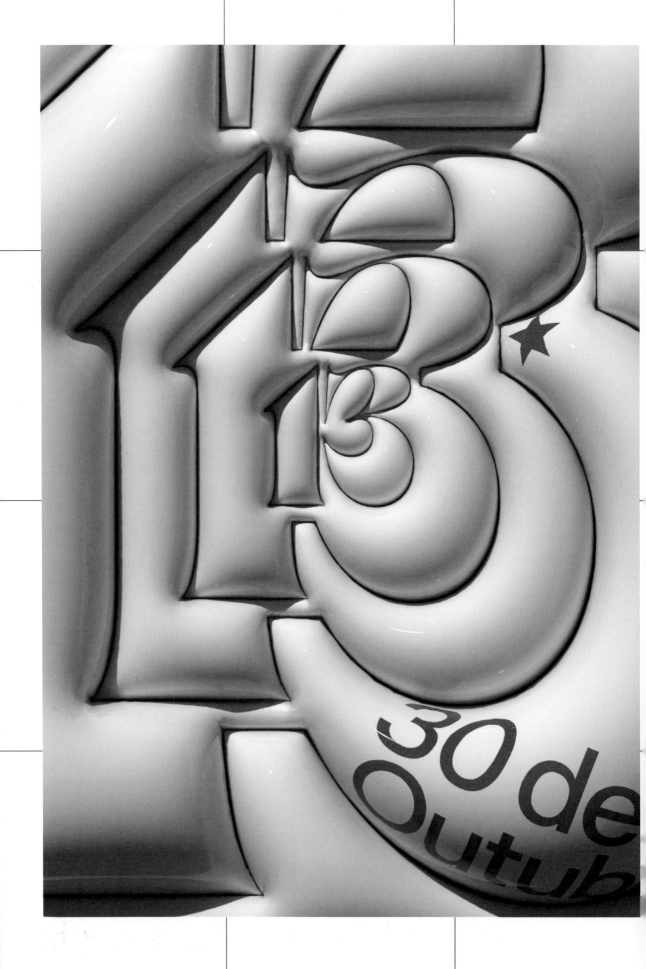

These posters were designed for the occasion of the 2022 Brazilian presidential elections. For designer Daniel Escudeiro it was, 'an incredibly important moment for Brazilian politics since this was the election in which the obtuse far-right incumbent Bolsonaro could finally be ousted'. '30 de Outubro' was the election runoff date and the number '13' was the voting code for president Lula. Escudeiro wanted to express, 'a sense of joy, festivity and enthusiasm', with these posters.

COMPANY
Daniel Escudeiro
URL
behance.net/danielescudeiro
FONTS
Antarctica
SOFTWARE
Adobe Creative Suite

Zuzanna Rogatty
Marc Urtasun
FOREAL
Everyday Practice
Baillat Studio

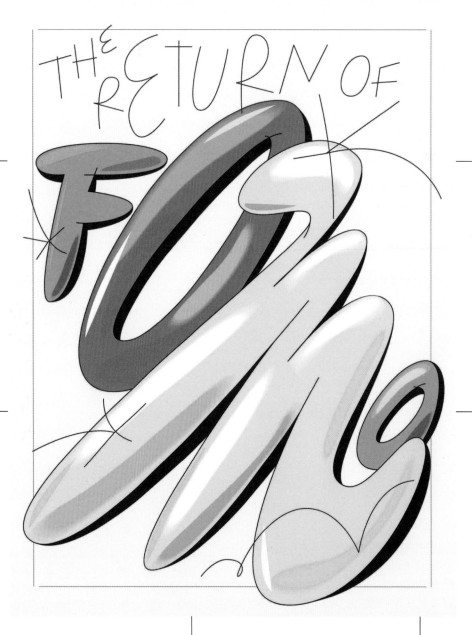

New York Magazine

COMPANY
Zuzanna Rogatty
CREATIVE DIRECTOR
Thomas Alberty
Ellen Peterson
URL
rogatty.com
FONTS
Custom
SOFTWARE
Adobe Illustrator

A series of typographic illustrations by Zuzanna Rogatty for the summer issue of 'New York Magazine' and its cover story 'The Return of FOMO. Our uneasy Great Opening'.

The series consists of the title lettering on the cover, five titles within the article and a set of secondary illustrations.

The phrase 'great times' tries to convey that life as a child is always better. Everything is simpler, everything makes you happier and the only worry is eating cotton candy at the fair.

Great Times

This illustration intends to make us think about childhood, using two main elements, typography and candy floss. The phrase 'great times' tries to convey that life as a child is always better. Everything is simpler, everything makes you happier and the only worry is eating cotton candy at the fair.

Just Keep Swimming

This work is intended to convey the idea of 'never stop trying'. The phrase is taken from the movie 'Finding Nemo' and the typography is inspired by the wavy shapes of the sea.

BOTH PROJECTS

COMPANY
Marc Urtasun
URL
marcurtasun.com
FONTS
Custom
SOFTWARE
Cinema 4D

Interview
Marc Urtasun

I started with curiosity and a passion for graffiti. Since I was a child, I liked to look at the walls of the streets, looking for letters.

marcurtasun.com

How would you describe your style and creative process?

→ I would describe my style as very direct, visual, colorful and pleasing on the eye. While my creative process always starts with a long period of thinking about the idea and meditating. When the idea takes shape, I do a lot of tests and discard many options. Then, little by little, only the best is left.

What inspired you to first incorporate 3D typography in your work?

→ I really like 3D because it allows you to make things that look real. It allows you to play with textures, colors and materials that impact much more than a 2D illustration. I like to create images that look like they can be touched, that make you want to get inside. I like the real world and that's why I like to use 3D. On the other hand, it is a way to create very powerful images that would be impossible in the real world, but we can make them real.

Can you walk us through your workflow when designing 3D type?

→ I usually start with a sketch on paper. Then I transfer it to Illustrator and work on it, mainly in black and white, to make sure it works and reads well. Then I pass it to 3D and start modeling the letters to give it the volume and shape needed. Finally, I make many tests of materials, colors, lighting... until I get the best image.

How do you choose the right 3D software for your typography projects?

→ I use Cinema 4D for the 3D and also Illustrator to make sure the sketch works well before modeling.

What are some of the challenges you face when designing 3D type?

→ Usually, the worst problems are problems related to technical things, computer problems, things that I want to do but I don't know how to do them. 3D is very technical and there are an infinite number of tools and problems that can arise. It is also a slow process and the render time is something I hate.

What do you see as the future of 3D typography in graphic design?
→   I don't think it is better or worse, or that it has to be used more or less. It simply has to be used well. The 3D cannot replace the 2D because it is totally different. In the future, I see it as something easier to use and more immediate.

How do you stay inspired?
→   Being curious. If you are curious, you always have things to do, to think, to try. There are many things to be inspired by, especially nature or animals, which are an infinite source of inspiration.

What are your goals for the future of your company?
→   My goal is to work more on physical things. Less digital. I'd like to make more sculptures and objects, for example.

HELL YEAH

This illustration talks about positivity, utilising a phrase as powerful as 'Hell yeah', combined with bright colours. The piece also works as a sculpture. It is modelled in 3D and there is also a physical version.

FONTS
Custom
SOFTWARE
Cinema 4D

Kalahari

The African-themed water
and amusement park Kalarhari
in Wisconsin, USA, contains some
'wild' water rides, which FOREAL
reflected for them in a bold
typographic key visual.

COMPANY
FOREAL
URL
weareforeal.com
FONTS
Custom
SOFTWARE
Cinema 4D
Octane Renderer
Adobe Photoshop

VIBE TREND Cover Design

Everyday Practice designed this series of playlist covers for NAVER music streaming platform VIBE. The design of the playlist TREND, which selects overseas music according to the genre, conveys the theme typographically and through graphics that symbolise each concept. Everyday Practice also tried to convey the genre and mood of each playlist through various colour combinations.

COMPANY
Everyday Practice
URL
everyday-practice.com
FONTS
Hrot
SOFTWARE
Adobe Photoshop
Adobe InDesign
Cinema 4D

The design of the playlist TREND, which selects overseas music according to the genre, conveys the theme typographically and through graphics that symbolise each concept.

Retina Magazine

This illustration is for a magazine that covers new technologies. The piece aims to communicate the concept of technology, but in a different and attractive way. Marc Urtasun was inspired by elastic, organic materials and the vibrant colours of nature.

COMPANY
Marc Urtasun
URL
marcurtasun.com
FONTS
Custom
SOFTWARE
Cinema 4D

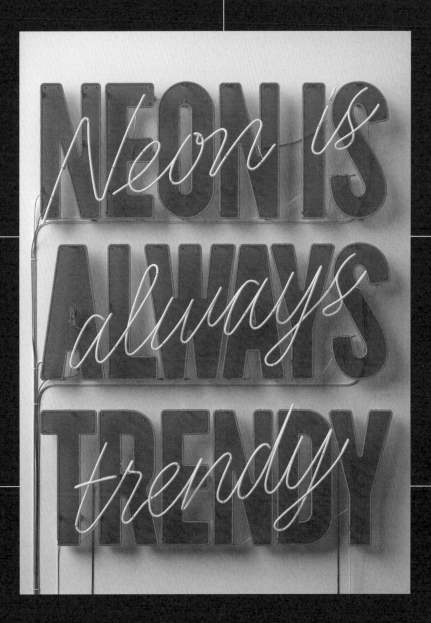

Neon is Always Trendy

The message is clear: Neon is always trendy. Designer Marc Urtasun is very interested in neon as a material and as an element to create text. Historically, it is a relatively old way of creating signs in all kinds of shapes. As our cities continuously change, the way of making corporate letters out of neon has always remained.

That's why Urtasun couldn't think of a better way than literally expressing this message with neon letters.

COMPANY
Marc Urtasun
URL
marcurtasun.com
FONTS
Inspired by Bebas
SOFTWARE
Cinema 4D

COMPANY
Baillat Studio
URL
baillatstudio.com
FONTS
Roobert
SOFTWARE
Adobe Illustrator
Adobe InDesign

Marché Shoni

For its second year, 'Marché Shoni', a festival celebrating the culture of the Shaughnessy Village neighbourhood, enlisted Baillat Studio to continue developing its visual identity. The year's theme continued the idea of bringing people together through a modular illustrative system. The illustrations were created with circular building blocks that come together to create type and visuals that express the light-hearted, bubbly and fun nature of the market.

ÉVÈNEMENTS
DE CETTE
SEMAINE

MARCHÉ
SHONI   (5)

SHUYI
TEALICIOUS (1)

234 rue St-Denis   Ⓜ Guy Concordia

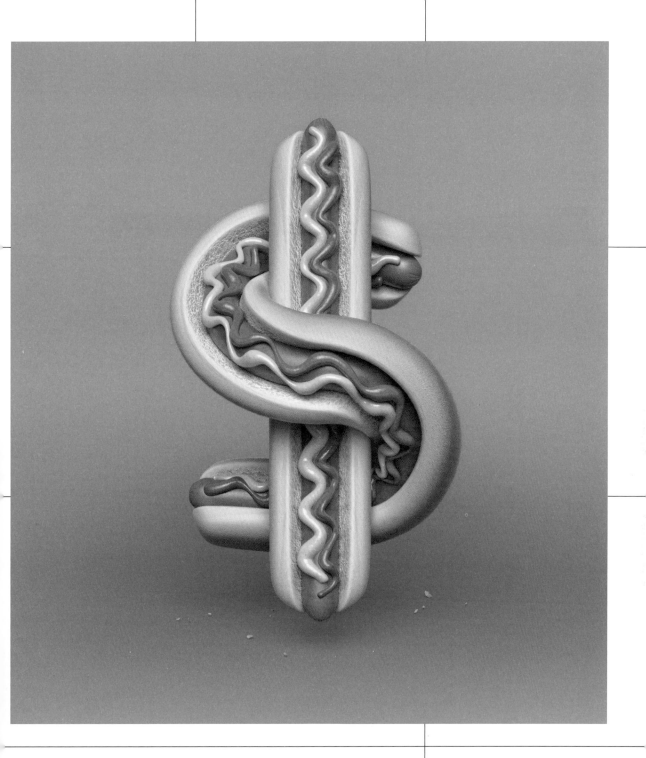

NYC Love Ice Cream
& Dollar Hot Dog

Part of a self-initiated illustration series by FOREAL, dedicated
to expressing their love for the dynamic spirit of New York City
and its iconic landmarks. This vibrant homage captures the essence
of a city that inspires creatives globally.

COMPANY
FOREAL
URL
weareforeal.com
FONTS
Custom
SOFTWARE
Cinema 4D
Octane Renderer
Adobe Photoshop

Sounds

Part of a large set of 3D
headlines for an advertising
campaign for Base, a renowned
German network provider.

COMPANY
FOREAL
URL
weareforeal.com
FONTS
Custom
SOFTWARE
Cinema 4D
Octane Renderer
Adobe Photoshop

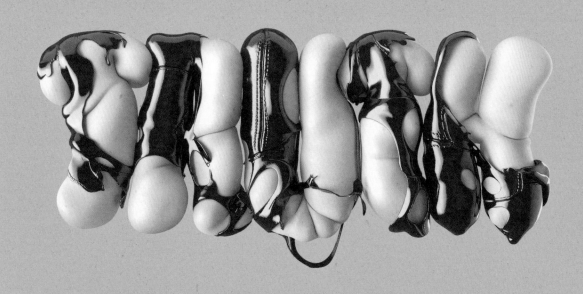

Truth AF

FOREAL teamed up with
Alex Trochut to create this
3D illustration as part of 'truth.
af' – an ongoing series of
typographic, animated one-
word poems.

COMPANY
FOREAL
URL
weareforeal.com
FONTS
Custom
SOFTWARE
Cinema 4D
Octane Renderer
Adobe Photoshop

138

Lo Siento
Snask
Adriana Mora/By Electra
Everyday Practice

Berlin Homage

This poster tribute by Lo Siento is for the Holocaust Memorial in Berlin. The design company constructed an uppercase letter 'B' from paper in a style reminiscent of the memorial. The poster was designed for an exhibition in Berlin, organised by Show Us Your Type.

Lettering - gewidmet den Holocaust-Mahnmal
Von Lo Siento

COMPANY
Lo Siento
URL
losiento.net
FONTS
Custom
SOFTWARE
Adobe Illustrator

COMPANY
Snask
URL
snask.com
FONTS
Custom
SOFTWARE
Adobe Creative Suite

Slanted

Snask was invited to make a poster for 'Slanted' magazine's 34th issue about the crisis in Europe. They decided to go for, 'the right wing blowing their extreme and rotten winds'.

DESIGNTIMES: Issue 63

Lo Siento worked with the concept of 'craft', turning the word into a handmade piece, made from paper. They then adapted the word 'craft' to fit the space available on the cover, so that it could fit perfectly, creating a condensed form of typography. They then went about giving the typography a sense of depth, creating the concept of a 'ladder to craft'. This was assembled and then photographed from various points.

The result gives us a group of images that adds meaning to the requested cover design.

COMPANY
Lo Siento
URL
losiento.net
FONTS
Custom
SOFTWARE
Adobe Illustrator

Studio Posters

Adriana Mora designed this series of posters as a continuation of a previous project. The use of extra-condensed typography, applied to an engineered print format, allows the designer to generate movement through folds, without losing legibility.

The choice of colour palette (inspired by the work of Stuart Davis) contrasts with the visually heavy elements, generating a harmony and playful dynamism.

The phrases used in these posters are part of a comical communication within the designer's studio.

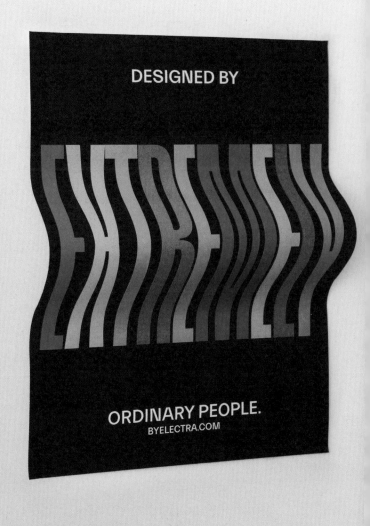

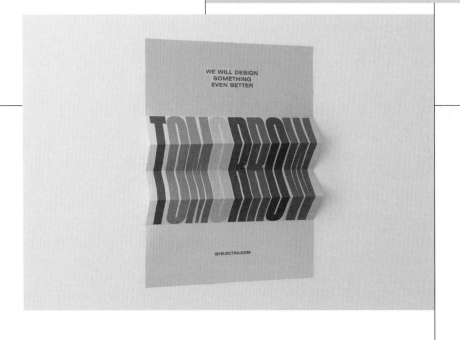

COMPANY
Adriana Mora/By Electra
URL
byelectra.com
FONTS
Druk
Grandmaster
Tower
Fixture Ultra
SOFTWARE
Adobe Creative Suite

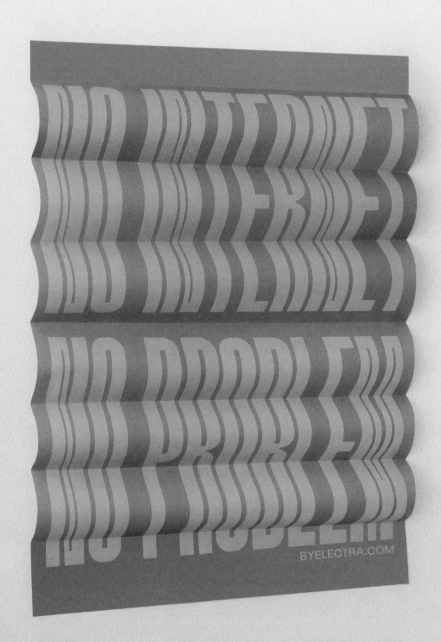
NO INTERNET NO PROBLEM!!!

BYELECTRA.COM

REPEAT AFTER ME:

WE HAVE DONE
THIS BEFORE

BYELECTRA.COM

The use of extra condensed typography applied to an engineered print format allows the designer to generate movement through folds, without losing legibility.

Everyday Practice created this poster design for the 'Weltformat Graphic Design Festival' in Lucerne, Switzerland. They designed a motion poster that shows the process of creating a single title by bringing together multiple objects in the office that are easily accessible in everyday life.

COMPANY
Everyday Practice
URL
everyday-
practice.com
FONTS
Ruder Plakat
SOFTWARE
None

FLOW

HYPE

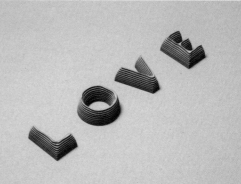

LOVE

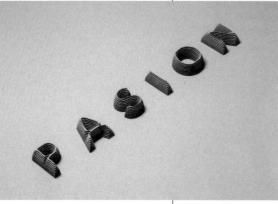

PASION

QUICK

COMPANY
Lo Siento
URL
losiento.net
FONTS
Helvetica Neue
SOFTWARE
Adobe Illustrator

Topographical: From Helvetica to Organica

This alphabet, made of layers of paper, creates a set of typographic topographies. The result of this, is a sans serif typography on one side and a topographic analogue version on the other side, or back of the piece, constructed by superimposing layers. Each letter is composed of a positive matrix (form) and a container of its counter-form.

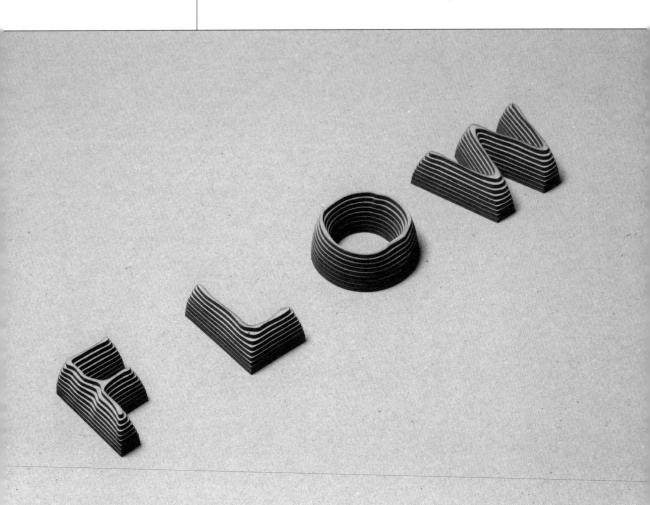

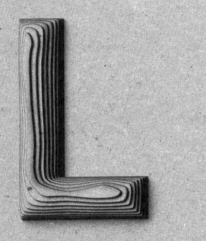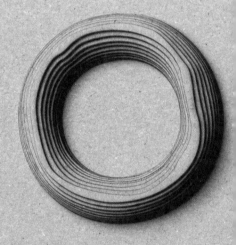

 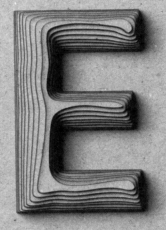

Fontwerk – Hamster

Concept and production by Snask for Fontwerk's new typeface 'Hamster'.

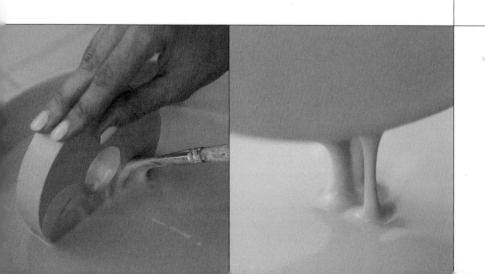

COMPANY
Snask
URL
snask.com
FONTS
Hamster
SOFTWARE
Adobe Creative Suite

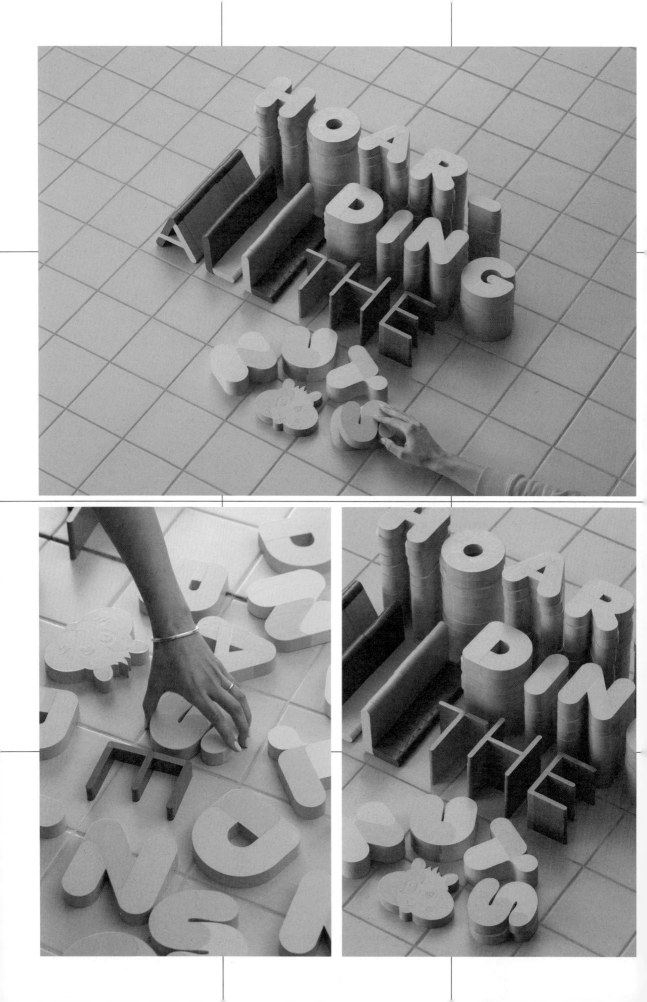

EMPO

Lo Siento designed this graphic identity for EMPO, a school and office specialising in psycho-emotional osteopathy.

The design studio took the human body and its constituent parts as the starting point for the graphic identity, using them to develop an exclusive alphabet for the project.

The outcome seeks to be reminiscent of organic forms. The human organs and typography were both made from coloured cardboard and the design is based on the Pythagorean theorem, which results in a three-dimensional polyhedral alphabet built entirely out of paper.

In 2010, the project was awarded with a Grand Laus (Spain's most important design award).

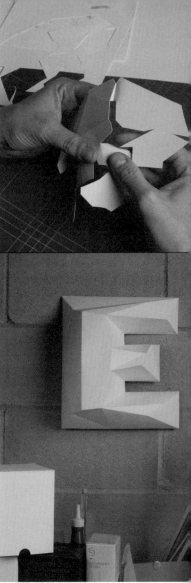

EMPO typeface

* Alfabeto realizado por formulación matemática basado en la fórmula de pitágoras:

Distancia real = Raíz cuadrada de la suma de los cuadrados de la diferencia entre coordenadas correspondientes

COMPANY
Lo Siento
URL
losiento.net
FONTS
Custom font based on
Pythagorean theorem
SOFTWARE
Adobe Illustrator

gràffica.

DISEÑO · CREATIVIDAD · CULTURA VISUAL

BRANDING

COMPANY
Lo Siento
URL
losiento.net
FONTS
Domaine Display Bold
SOFTWARE
Adobe Illustrator

Gràffica

Cover for the magazine 'Gràffica', entirely designed and assembled layer-by-layer to achieve a three-dimensional, typographic object, which was then photographed.

COMPANY
Lo Siento
URL
losiento.net
FONTS
Deko Blakk
SOFTWARE
Adobe Illustrator

WAM (We Are Mono)

This series of covers was created for a rock band from Barcelona. The initial concept is based on the creation of a purely geometric typography that goes from flat to three-dimensional. It has been constructed by hand on white cardboard and then it has been transformed by applying coloured paint on several of its letters. As a result, several covers have been created with different compositions of shape and colour.

The initial concept is based on the creation of a purely geometric typography that goes from flat to three-dimensional.

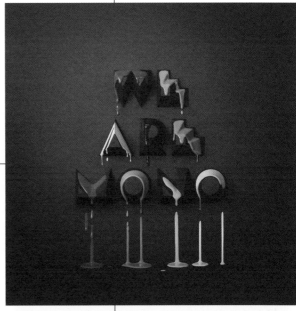

168

Ariane Spanier
Hust Wilson
FOREAL
Mario De Meyer
Matteo Campostrini
Andrew Footit
Julia Miceli Pitta
Marc Urtasun
A New Kind Of Kick

Year of Language

Typographic design for a series of installations in public spaces called 'Language explosions' within the 'Year of Language 2022' at the Klassikstiftung Weimar – a foundation that archives and hosts classical literature and art in the city of Weimar.

Quotes by the authors were spread out on three-dimensional objects and a room was filled entirely with poems by Goethe on the walls and floor. People could take a walking tour following the installations, read the sculptures, sit and rest on them. The writings were picked regarding their connection and value to contemporary matters, human sensitivities and politics.

COMPANY
Ariane Spanier
**3D DESIGN
& PRODUCTION
MANAGEMENT**
Franke Steinert
URL
arianespanier.com
FONTS
Walbaum Pro
SOFTWARE
Adobe Illustrator

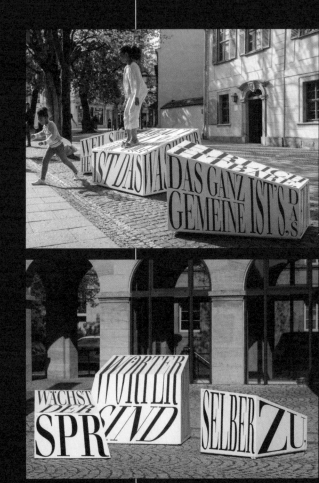

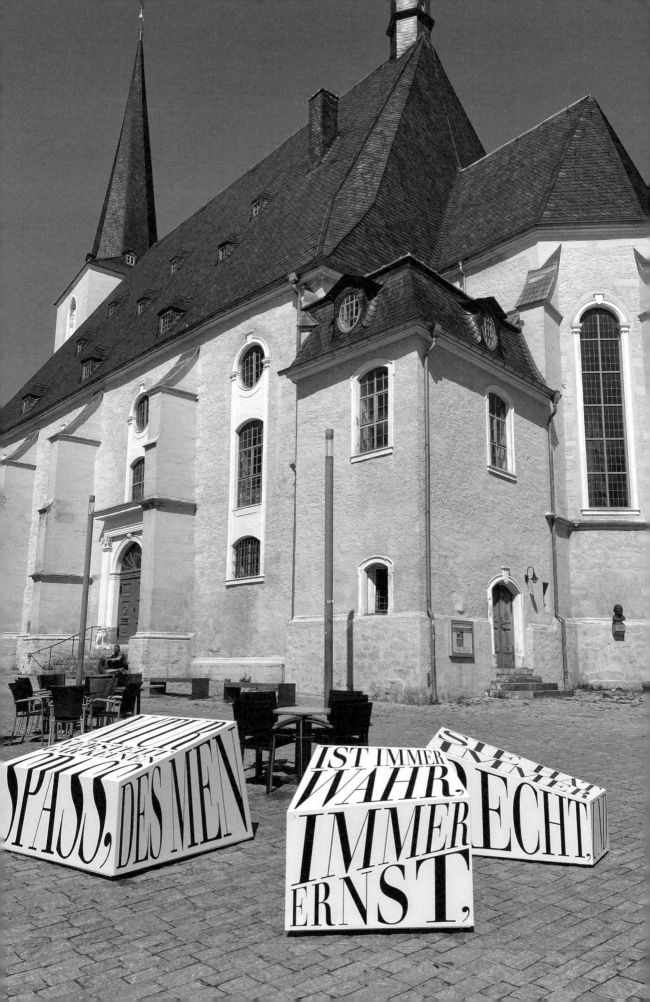

Interview
Hust Wilson

In the year 2013 I started volunteering at a local church, which led me to designing posters for the youth department every week. I spent my time at the church for five years until I decided to venture into an advertising agency, with the help of a friend. I got promoted as Art Director after being there for six months. Three years later at the agency, I decided to go full time as a freelancer and the rest is history as they say.

hustwilson.com

How would you describe your style and creative process?
→   I would describe my style as bold and colorful, with grain texture applied to extruded letters. I love creating bold compositions that bring an emotional feeling to it. I find that if I don't have a connection with my own design, I can't expect others to feel the same way about it.

What inspired you to first incorporate 3D typography in your work?
→   I remember trying different techniques as I began my journey into lettering, but they felt too flat for me and did not bring any feeling to the design and I felt like I was trying to be someone I am not. I began enjoying the journey of starting from nothing and seeing how any project I work on comes alive.

Can you walk us through your workflow when designing 3D typography?
→   I enjoy starting my process in Procreate, as I find that I can work on quick, rough sketches before fully committing to the design. I would then clean up my rough sketches and transfer my sketch to Adobe Illustrator. From here on, I would vectorise my shapes and play around with color, I would normally go to Adobe Color for inspiration. I love giving clients color options, aside from the normal colors I would use for my personal projects. Once the vector work is set, I import my design into Adobe Photoshop and work on adding grain with the filter gallery and finalize in Procreate, with final details and grain texture.

WIRED: BIG TECH'S PLEDGE TO BLACK AMERICA

Cover design for the November 2021 issue of 'WIRED' magazine. The cover story is about HOPE Credit Union, which is a black-owned, small financial firm that helped small businesses stay afloat during the pandemic. Netflix announced it would deposit $10 million to the credit union, so the story dives into Netflix's overall arrangement to put 2% of its cash reserves into black banks, and the behind-the-scenes story and real-world impact of the deal.

FREEDOM TO BE

Project created for Doyle Dayn Bernbach (DDB) with the help of Hust Wilson's agents The Different Folk.

BOTH PROJECTS

FONTS
Custom
SOFTWARE
Procreate
Adobe Illustrator
Adobe Photoshop

I find that if I don't have a connection with my own design, I can't expect others to feel the same way about it.

Do you use any 3D software in your typography projects?

→ Depending on the projects, I would use Cinema 4D and Nomad Sculpt for the iPad. Sometimes it helps for me to understand perspective and different ways of doing things that would help when sketching.

What are some of the challenges you face when designing 3D type?

→ The challenge I face, is working on compositions that have longer words. I find when sketching, I have to try and blend shapes that involve the extrusion of each letter, so that I can have a composition that compliments the design. For Instagram, I often end up creating a carousel to challenge myself on longer compositions.

What do you see as the future of 3D typography in graphic design?

→ With technology enhancing, I find that 3D has become more popular over the years. Anyone has access to learning 3D software online in the comfort of their home. As we move forward, we would probably want to scale them up to larger sizes, besides murals. Maybe large sculptures, architecture, AR, who knows. I think it's an exciting time for all of us and the generation to come.

How do you stay inspired?

→ There's times where I would jump into it without thinking about a concept or how it will look at the end. Over the years, I promised myself to never repost a design on social media but challenge myself to work on a new design every time I had the chance. There are days where I feel like my brain does not want to function at all. In these times, self love and self care is important. Spending time away from my desk helps me to recoup and enjoy life and be inspired when I get back.

What are your goals for the future of your company?

→ Our goals are to move into the fashion, tattoo and mural industry. I find that there has been so much potential for my work to be recognized in those other fields. But one step at a time, no rush to it though, because I find that it's great to gain more knowledge and learn about any passion you would like to pursue.

SELF EXPRESSION

Hust Wilson was invited by Pentagram to do a half-page, typographic illustration of the quote, 'Think about how to harness self-expression', for 'Wharton' magazine.

FONTS
Custom
SOFTWARE
Procreate
Adobe Illustrator
Adobe Photoshop

ABOUT HOW TO HARNESS

Forbes Spain

Hust Wilson was invited by Forbes Spain to illustrate the words, 'Las 75 mejores empresas para trabajar' (The 75 best companies to work for).

COMPANY
Hust Wilson
URL
hustwilson.com
FONTS
Custom
SOFTWARE
Procreate
Adobe Illustrator
Adobe Photoshop

COMPANY
FOREAL
URL
weareforeal.com
FONTS
Custom
SOFTWARE
Cinema 4D
Octane Renderer
Adobe Photoshop

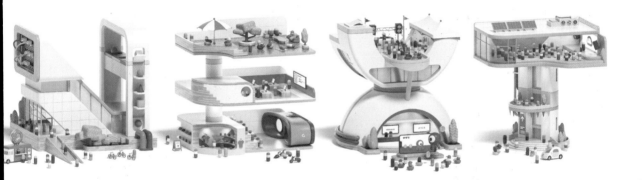

Google Next

FOREAL teamed up with the agency VSA to create 36 animated visuals for Google's biggest conference: Google Next in San Francisco in 2019. Their key visuals served as the visual design of the entire conference.

MONDAY, 20 JUNE, 15:00, GRAND ADITORIUM
STEFAN SAGMEISTER & BILLIE WHITEHOUSE

Today, people are interacting with brands in radically new ways. But meaningful experiences depend as much as ever on empathy, thoughtful design and risk taking. Join us for a seminar on connecting with audiences, inspiring awe, and changing games.

ART BY
MARIO DE MEYER

Adobe
Cannes
Lions –
Experience

Mario De Meyer was commissioned by Adobe to create a visual for the 'Experience' seminar at Cannes Lions. The seminar explored how risk-taking and fighting against industry norms are critical to delivering breakthrough experiences.

The Great
Gatsby/
Deluxe
Edition –
Penguin
Books

In this reworking of an American classic, the goal was to, 'take the cover design into the 21st century and make something very different, unique with a modern twist'. The book cover is printed in four Pantone colours.

BOTH PROJECTS

COMPANY
Mario De Meyer
URL
dm2graphics.com
FONTS
Custom
SOFTWARE
Adobe Illustrator

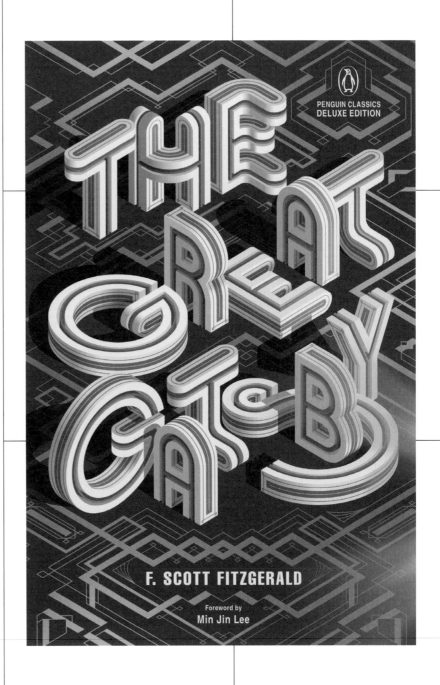

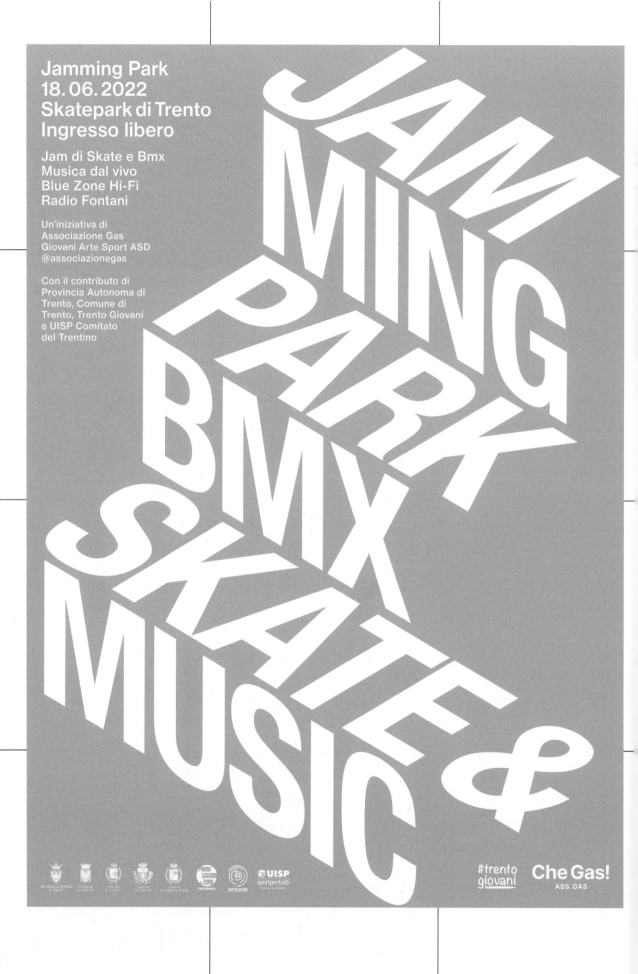

Jamming Park
18.06.2022
Skatepark di Trento
Ingresso libero

Jam di Skate e Bmx
Musica dal vivo
Blue Zone Hi-Fi
Radio Fontani

Un'iniziativa di
Associazione Gas
Giovani Arte Sport ASD
@associazionegas

Con il contributo di
Provincia Autonoma di
Trento, Comune di
Trento, Trento Giovani
e UISP Comitato
del Trentino

JAM
MING
PARK
BMX
SKATE
MUSIC &

#trento
giovani

Che Gas!
ASS. GAS

Jamming Park

'Jamming Park' is a live-event at the skatepark in the city of Trento, in the North of Italy. It is organised once a year by the volunteers of the non-profit association Associazione Gas and involves skateboarding, BMX, cooking and live music.

　　Trento's skatepark has been recently renewed and enlarged, becoming one of Italy's largest playground for such sports. The poster series is inspired by Trento's famous and widely appreciated stair-set, which socially and sportingly gathers skaters, bikers and friends of all communities. In addition to the printed and animated posters, a small run of screenprinted t-shirts were designed and given away for free on the day of the event.

COMPANY
Matteo Campostrini
URL
matteocampostrini.com
FONTS
Helvetica
SOFTWARE
Adobe Illustrator
Adobe InDesign
Adobe After Effects

The poster series is inspired by Trento's famous and widely appreciated stair-set, which socially and sportingly gathers skaters, bikers and friends of all communities.

A short version of my story. I became involved in graphic design quite early on, straight out of high school I interned for a small studio for free for two months. I then worked full time for that studio for a year or so then moved on to a corporate, in-house design team and from there moved to larger advertising agencies before going independent. I am self-taught, so during all of my years of full time working, I would come home and work on personal projects into the early morning hours, teaching myself software, experimenting and working on new techniques to further my skills.

andrewfootit.com

THE NEW YORK TIMES – FOR KIDS

A front cover illustration for 'The New York Times – For Kids'. This issue was based around the theme 'Back to School' and topics related to school. Andrew Footit created the pencils in Illustrator and built up the layers in Photoshop, as well as the type. The type has a slight bevelling, to give it a de-bossed look, as you would get on real pencils.

FONTS
Custom
SOFTWARE
Adobe Illustrator
Adobe Photoshop

How would you describe your style and creative process?

→ My process is very experimental. I spend a lot of time experimenting and exploring what works and what does not for most projects, this can sometimes result in some pretty nice accidents. My style involves the use of a lot of colour and texture, so it needs to be balanced and I also need to know when to hold back with colour and texture. I like to add depth to what I create, so most of my work has elements of depth to it, whether it is 3D type or shapes with depth.

What inspired you to first incorporate 3D typography in your work?

→ The first bigger advertising agency I worked for was more of a production and animation agency, so most of the work I produced had 3D elements to it. I really enjoyed my work going from flat vector-based shapes into 3D, it added so much more depth and life to my work. I started learning 3D software and started adding more 3D to my process.

Can you walk us through your workflow when designing 3D type?

→ This all depends on the finish I want for the work. If it is more of a graphic, vector style, then I will sketch and experiment in Adobe Illustrator. If it's a more polished finish, with more realism, then I work in Cinema 4D. I still work on rough compositions for the typography, but I will experiment and render the final artwork from Cinema 4D. I still like my 3D work to have a more graphic style, so this will come through in the textures and materials I use.

The New York Times

For Kids

EDITORS' NOTE: THIS

SECTION SHOULD NOT BE READ BY GROWN-UPS

PLEASE SAY MY NAME
CORRECTLY!
PAGE 11

A DAY WITH DIABETES
PAGE 4

CARTWHEEL
THROUGH SPACE
PAGE 4

HOW TO START A
SCHOOL NEWSPAPER
PAGE 6

SPLAT!
IT'S BUG HUNTING TIME
PAGE 3

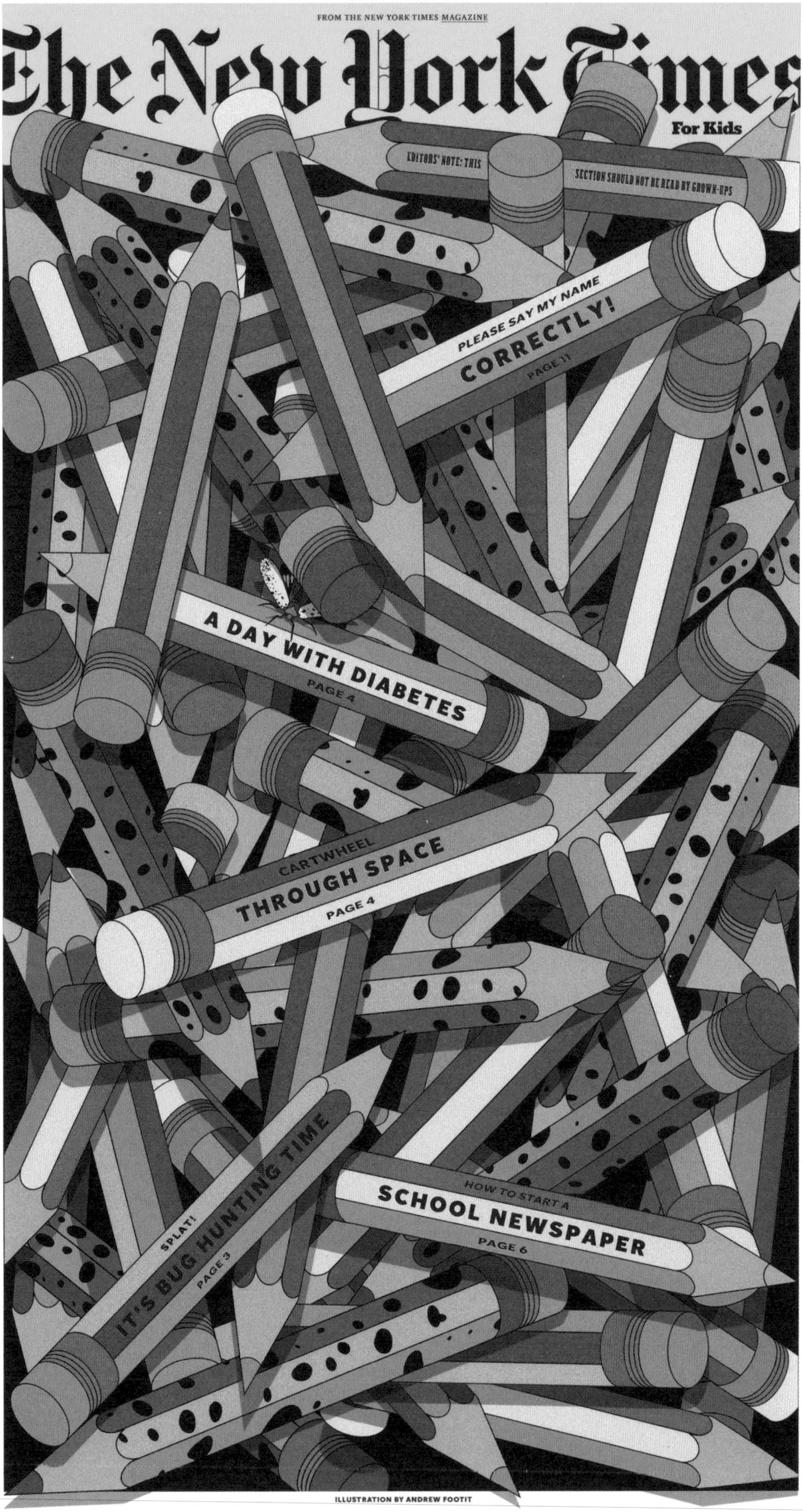

ILLUSTRATION BY ANDREW FOOTIT

**ART BASEL MIAMI – LIZZO
X AMERICAN EXPRESS**

Andrew Footit was commissioned,
along with two other artists, to
create illustrated type of song lyrics
for Lizzo's performance at Art Basel
in Miami. The typography was
animated for the stage screens during
the song and posters of each artist's
typography were sold during the
Art Basel event.

Do you use any 3D software in your typography projects?

→ I use Cinema 4D and Adobe Illustrator to create all my typographic work. Which software I use on each project is down to the style that a client wants or if it's a personal project I mix it up.

What are some of the challenges you face when designing 3D type?

→ You can be quite playful with 3D type and I feel you can have a lot of flexibility with it, so I don't run into many challenges apart form lighting and materials, but this can vary from project to project. Often, what you initially wanted to work on, as a direction, may change due to a client wanting multiple variations in layout orientations. So, what works really well for a landscape layout, does not work well for portrait, or it needs to be scaled down or broken up.

What do you see as the future of 3D typography in graphic design?

→ I feel a big shift will be coming in future towards VR/AR. I think more demand will be coming for 3D work in VR worlds. With the release and development of more and more VR products, this will increase demand for more work to translate into these virtual worlds. If creatives are not working in 3D yet, I think it would be a positive move to add 3D to your skill set and workflow.

How do you stay inspired?

→ For me, staying inspired comes from various sources. It can come from books – seeing what other creatives are up to can give you creative ideas, whether its new software or a new technique in creating something. For me, it also comes from working a lot on personal projects, where you just take time to play and be creative without constraints to work within.

What are your goals for the future of your company?

→ I have quite a few goals I would like to achieve. I have quite a few clients and brands I would like to work with still and I also want to create more physical products and experiences. This could be installations or products in fashion and interior products.

FONTS
Custom
SOFTWARE
Adobe Illustrator
Adobe Photoshop

Libre

'Libre' is a film festival. The event is a collective space for developing and discussing visual practices and their contexts through documentary films, critical readings, and meetings with curators and diverse creators.

Julia Miceli Pitta's work for the identity began with the idea of how light is seen from a projector. Whether in a movie theater or at home, the light has a certain direction. They started drawing lines with this concept in mind. Also, the festival will take place in the middle of a lagoon, so flexibility, liquidity and motion are some of the characteristics that have been conveyed.

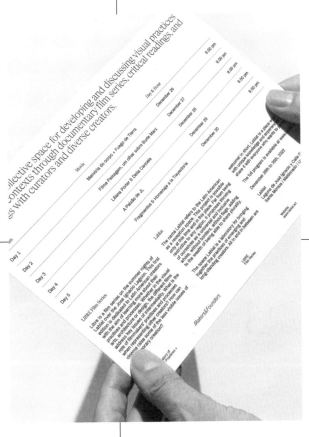

COMPANY
Julia Miceli Pitta
URL
juliamicelipitta.com
FONTS
Big Daily
Sempione Grotesk
SOFTWARE
Cinema 4D
Adobe Photoshop

COMPANY
Marc Urtasun
URL
marcurtasun.com
FONTS
Custom
SOFTWARE
Cinema 4D

Viva la Velocity

This illustration is made for the Nike brand and the Chelsea team. The illustration is for the Spanish player 'Pedro' and had to represent him. Pedro is from Tenerife, an island in the Canary Islands. That's why the fluid shapes remind us of the water and the sea.

Hyundai N

This set of typographic illustrations was designed for Hyundai N's online platforms. Hyundai N is know for its high-performance and motorsport vehicles. They collaborate with artists to create work for their social media pages which can also be downloaded by their audience as screen wallpapers.

These illustrations were animated and had sound effects added to create a sense of speed and handling.

COMPANY
Andrew Footit
URL
andrewfootit.com
FONTS
Custom
SOFTWARE
Adobe Illustrator
Adobe Photoshop
Adobe After Effects

01 Ally CAPELLINO AW20
"Twitching"

Future Nature

This identity, by A New Kind Of Kick, is for a new world communications agency, with a focus on B Corp and responsible brands. The brief was to show care for the planet, while avoiding any cliches. The design agency created a logo around the idea of an invisible globe, to reflect this planet-first approach.

COMPANY
A New Kind Of Kick
URL
anewkindofkick.com
FONTS
GT Alpina Light
MaisonNeue Book
SOFTWARE
Adobe Illustrator
Adobe InDesign
Adobe After Effects

RESOURCES ++ MOBILITY ++ EQUITY ++ RESOURCES

EUROPAN
EUROPAN
EUROPAN
EUROPAN
EUROPAN

15

NORWAY

RAUFOSS
RAUFOSS
RAUFOSS

RØDBERG
RØDBERG
RØDBERG
RØDBERG

CITIES

GUOVDAGEAIDNU
GUOVDAGEAIDNU
GUOVDAGEAIDNU
GUOVDAGEAIDNU

PRODUCTIVE
PRODUCTIVE
PRODUCTIVE
PRODUCTIVE
PRODUCTIVE
PRODUCTIVE

RESOURCES ++ MOBILITY ++ EQUITY ++ RESOURCES

Europan Norway 15

Graphic identity for the 15th edition of the Norwegian section of 'Europan' – an architecture competition for young, urban and architectural design professionals. The session on 'Productive Cities 2' looked at synergies between ecosystems, biotopes and artefacts, between functions and uses and between citizens in Norwegian towns in rural areas. The design concept played on machinery and typography rolling on cylinders machines.

COMPANY
Ariane Spanier
URL
arianespanier.com
FONTS
Aperçu
SOFTWARE
Adobe Illustrator
Adobe After Effects
Adobe InDesign

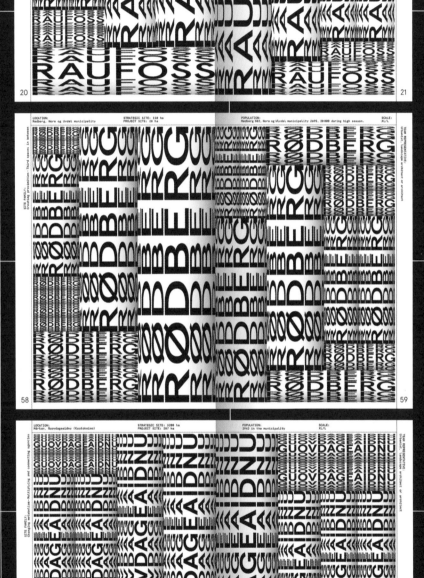

200

© 2024 Counter-Print
counter-print.co.uk
info@counter-print.co.uk

First published in the
United Kingdom in 2024.

ISBN:
978-1-915392-10-7

**British Library cataloguing-
in-publication data:
A catalogue of this
book can be found
in the British Library.**

Print:
1010 Printing International
Limited, China.

Cover Design:
Atelier Baudelaire x
Clément Frassi, based
on a project developed
with Jérémie Harper
(GeneralPublic) in 2017 for
the Salon de Montrouge.

Spread Design:
Counter-Print

Typeface:
Practical Grotesk